Rob Suggs captures the crazy passion of Southern football, and particularly the roller coaster emotions of following the Georgia Bulldogs. Sometimes all you've got is laughter—and the supply of that never runs dry in Sax Attacks.
Mark Schlabach. ESPN

Opens with a fascinating, funny account of how the advent of the Internet gave voice to the most important group of people in sports: the fans. You'll definitely laugh and even accidentally learn some stuff.
Matt Stinchcomb, SEC Network

The soothsaying of The Prophet Ooga, Rob's unwashed Internet alter ego, is just the tip of the proverbial iceberg. Did I mention Rob Suggs is a funny man? Sit back, preferably with a cold beverage and something red, black and comforting nearby, and enjoy.
Senator Blutarsky, Get the Picture

Even those who aren't Georgia fans will appreciate how Rob chronicles the history of the DawgVent from its humble beginnings to what it is now: the primary source of news and conversation for the most devoted Dawg fans.
Dan Wolken, USA TODAY

Suggs deftly picks up where the great Lewis Grizzard left off, with comedy, sarcasm, and insight.
Radi Nabulsi, UGASports.com

Be Sure to Read These Other Great Saxondawg Titles

50 Shades of Gray: A History of Dawg Britches
Doo Doo Ice: The Sanford Stadium Cookbook
99 Sanford Stadium Toilet-Waiting Activities
Penn Wagers and His Magic Yellow Hanky
Georgia's Historic Bogart: More than a Potty Stop
Handoff! A Life of Buck Belue
Honkin' and Cussin': Legendary Postgame Traffic Jams
of the Georgia Bulldogs
Tennessee's Most Thrilling Championships of Life
The Six-Day Auburn Miracle Diploma Plan
Reggie Ball's Thanksgiving Memories

SAX ATTACKS!

The Best of Saxondawg

On the Dawgvent

Illustrated

by Muttley

Illustrations © 2017 Joe D. Suggs
Cover design and interior design by Rob Suggs
Text Copyright © 2017 Rob Suggs
ISBN: 1548353442
ISBN-13: 978-1548353445

This book is dedicated to the rowdiest, funniest, most opinionated, most obsessive, the stubbornest, nastiest, most generous, most relentless, and above all, the most entertainingly addictive pack of yapping, unhouse-broken, play-call-questioning, net-surfing Dawgs ever to hunker. Long may they bark; and may the fireplugs, flora, and shrubberies along their paths runneth over forever.

Contents

Foreword i

D. G. D. Roll Call ii

The Life and Times of the Dawgvent.......................... 2

Thanks for the Game Day Wedding!............................37

Ooga Makes an Entrance 41

The Curious Adventure of the Black Stripe 44

NOTES FROM AROUND THE SEC 48

Ooga vs. Clemson, 2002 54

An Interview with Brian VanGorder 57

I Know Where You Sat Last Season 62

Ooga vs. South Carolina, 2002 68

Recrootin' Targets...70

Ooga's BYE Week...72

TECHWAD: A Visit to the Huddle 75

Obsessive Fixation Diary 79

Ooga vs. Northwestern State, 2002 83

Greg Blue Knocks USC QB Into Next Week.................85

The Jacket-Hater's Alphabet...88

Ooga vs. Alabama, 2002 90

Scrimmagin' with the Ol' Ball Coach 93

UGA's Absolutely Perfect Day: Hour by Hour...........98

Jacket Game Day! You Can Do That! 102

Ooga vs. Tennessee, 2002 107

Chicken Shop Closeout Sale... 110

Letter to Richt from the Omniscient Fanboy 113

Richt's Reply to the Omniscient Fanboy 117

Ooga Quickie 120

For Visiting Gamecocks: Hazardous Conditions Warning 121

Ooga vs. Kentucky, 2002 125

Meanwhile, on North Avenue.......................................127

Ooga's List: Top Ten Reeking Hordes 132

Ooga vs. Florida, 2002..133

Don't Run Down Clemson..136

An Ooga Thanksgiving 141

Ooga vs. Auburn, 2002 143

Certificate of Ownership 146

Greenbacks for Cam 149

Ooga vs. Georgia Tech, 2002.....................................153

Fresh Air for Olde Mist...156

Ooga vs. the Georgia Dome, 2002 160

Ooga's Kirbaic Prophecy 162

A Visit from St. Nick 166

How'd You Like a Nicholls Sandwich? 169

Next Week Is Misery 173

Ole Mist: A View from the Ledge.................................176

Tennessee: Guy Walks Into a Bar 178

Generic Gamecocks Column..180

Nerd-Whipped 184

Auburn: Banana Republic..189

Advanced Philosophy: The Tornado Game.........................193

Epilogue: It's a Hail Mary, Charlie Brown! 195

About the Author 201

Foreword

BY THE HON. SENATOR BLUTARSKY

From the Great State of Blogistan

You don't have to be Jewish to have a sense of humor, but it helps" is a saying I heard long ago.

As a long-suffering member of the collaborative effort known as Dawgnation—surely the interminable wait since enjoying a national title, as the culmination of a glorious 1980 season, qualifies as our own version of wandering in the desert—I can testify that pearl of wisdom applies equally to being a Georgia football fan.

"Michael" aka "The Senator" aka "QBR Jesus"

Did I mention that Rob Suggs is a funny man?

Anyone who, like me, has been plugged into the Georgia sports online community for a couple of decades has surely been entertained by the soothsaying of The Prophet Ooga, Rob's unwashed Internet alter ego. And that's just the tip of the proverbial iceberg, as you're about to have the pleasure of discovering.

So sit back, preferably with a cold beverage and something red, black and comforting nearby, and enjoy.

After all, that sense of humor helps.

Michael
www.blutarsky.wordpress.com/

D. G. D. Roll Call

Without the following Damn Good Dawgs, this book couldn't have happened. Okay, that's a lie. It could have happened, but it would just have been kind of lousy.

Particularly the first chapter, the part with all the history. Pretty much everything in that one would be made up, like the rest of the book. I'd be trying to tell you the Vent was made by little elves in a hollow tree, that the Germans did in fact bomb Pearl Harbor, and that Pluto-Centurion was a character in Star Trek.

But due to the following Damn Good, or in one or two cases, just Darn Good Dawgs, only about thirty to thirty-five percent of that chapter is made up.

Among the Vent's founders and caretakers, the following were particularly helpful in giving me the lowdown: Jason Brooks; Charly Pou; Vin Moscardelli; Wade; Steve Patterson; Radi Nabulsi.

Among those who read and endorsed this book, I'm grateful to the following: Matt Wolken; Mark Schlabach; Matt Stinchcomb; Chip Towers; The Hon. Senator Blutarsky.

For the thousands of words of columns and curiosities here, I'd like to thank my wife, Gayle, and my son, L'il Ooga the Second for serving as Laff-o-meters as I read aloud. It helped me decide what was funny and what just plain strange and uncalled-for. Gayle helped proofread. Radi encouraged me along the way and helped connect me to endorsers.

Lastly, if not for the Vent community, I'd have been writing for nobody. Which might have caused concern, and gotten me locked up by now in a place with a sunny veranda and where every Tuesday is Jello Night. And where you have to get past people even crazier than you to score a little Internet time.

The Life and Times of the Dawgvent

Jason Brooks was a young engineer from Cherokee High in Canton, Georgia. Class of '85, Go Warriors!

During the early nineties, people from the Class of '85 were still young folks. Sadly, that's no longer true. And some of them have really let themselves go, as you know if you've been to the reunions.

Anyway, Jason had picked up his computer skills at Southern Polytechnic. But now, in the Year of Our Lord 1996, he was a network engineer at Honeywell, a large international corporation that was a player in aerospace as well as home control systems.

These were the early days of computers, and the Internet was The Next Big Thing among the nerd community—of which

Honeywell, of course, had quite a few. In 1996, when Jason was still relatively young, as opposed to today, when, it must be admitted, he is not—he began to hear the chatter from interns.

At first, their statements about a "World Wide Web" sounded like a Dungeons and Dragons scenario. But as it turned out, this was a real thing, or *virtually* real—you found it in a place called "cyberspace." Which, again, was not what it sounded like. Jason had his doubts—nerds tell you a lot of things—but he was assured on good authority this was real.

Nerds, they insisted, were finally going to *rule*, for the first time, like ever. The geek would inherit the earth, one squalling, honking modem at a time.

Quickly, Jason Googled it. No, wait. We're talking about 1996. He apparently went to something called a library (I had to Google *that*), or perhaps consulted nerdish periodicals and back alley sages. Ultimately he installed on his computer the early browser known as Netscape.

In those days, Netscape was the going thing for visiting the messy but far-flung experiment known as the World Wide Web. Messy? The Internet was often described as "all the books of the world's libraries in one place—with the pages ripped out and scattered across the floor!" An amazing amount of stuff was there, but to find it, you really had to be diligent and ready to scan.

If you were there, you're nodding your head.

Jason found himself checking out the early web pages, which amounted to pioneer settlements on the digital prairie, and soon the fever was upon him. This was amazing! Anyone anywhere could be creative and publish a site about any subject he or she chose. He could create a "home page" of his own. But what about? Cool cars? Tribute to his faithful dog? Spice Girls? The Macarena?

No way—this was Jason Brooks, and his passion was *Georgia football*.

He could find almost nothing about that subject on the Web, and he knew there were about 93,000 other people who were as passionate about the Dawgs as he was.

He'd seen these like-minded souls in their native habitat, Sanford Stadium. They tended to be boisterous, dedicated, and red-clad. But there had to be a few of them who owned computers, right? Sure, not as many as the Georgia Tech fans, who were already ahead of the game, often posting tiny little graphics instead of just text, and tossing off mysterious acronyms such as "LOL" and "ROFLMAO."

There was already a Dawg site in existence: Dawgs Online, hosted by someone strangely known as Groo. Clearly an intelligent personage (there weren't too many certifiable dummies on the Internet in those days), Groo was writing his own content, in other words, "blogging," though the word didn't even exist yet. (It was a casual compression of "web log.") Jason didn't consider himself a writer, so exactly what kind of site should be pursue?

Not recruiting. That was a whole other kettle of fish, and to go that way, you had to be a little obsessed. The college football recruiting cottage industry went back to those who snipped little articles about "the state's blue chippers" from newspapers in the 1960s; then, the early 1980s, when a hobbyist named Joe Terranova, a Ford Motors executive, began keeping track of all-state football players across the nation.

He had the perfect football name—Joe TerraNOVA, baby!—and began publishing a newsletter and was shocked at how many people were out there who shared his interest.

In time, there were paid 1-900 phone lines with recruiting information, with actual people paying actual money to hear the rather generic info. All of it was national—you had to listen through all kinds of stuff about Notre Dame, you had to understand non-Southern dialects, and there was absolutely nothing you could do about that part.

You had to wonder—what if someone specialized in your region? Even just your team?

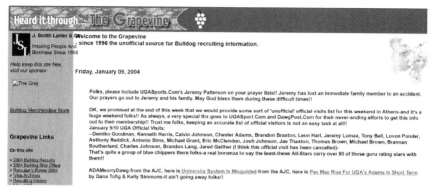

Table 1 Georgia Grapevine, January 9, 2004

Computin' Recruitin'

Charly Pou, who worked with the University of Georgia, was another early adopter of the computer craze—and another one who gazed at his computer, as he did at other things, and thought, "Hmmm. Football."

He recalls an Ohio State fan known to aficionados as Buckeye Dennis—a very nice guy, as Charly remembers him, regardless of OSU affinity. Dennis seems to have been one of the first in cyberspace to cover college football recruiting, with a site called the National Recruiting Center. It amounted to listening out for rumors from across America and posting them on his site. This had tremendous advantages to 1-900 numbers, obviously (such as being free if you owned a computer). Naturally, this took off, and the users were realizing they could create their own team-specific sites.

One of those was "The Unofficial University of Georgia Recruiting Page," a labor of love for an Emory Masters and Ph.D. candidate (UGA '91) named Vin Moscardelli. Many of these names, of the "founding fathers" of the Vent, aren't well known today—at least in this venue. There are no statues in cyberspace. But Vin was a pioneer in Dawg recruiting news online. He's now a political science prof at the University of Connecticut and still a true Dawg fan.

His page, the first draft of what became the Grapevine, then, was hosted on Emory University servers. And much of his early work was simply rehashing what the Atlanta sports page was saying, for whomever out there was listening. But as with so many of the early recruiting sites, sources began to materialize. One of these was Charly Pou, who, being in Athens, could at least offer what the Banner-Herald had to say.

And sometimes he had a bit more. He was one of those people so addicted to recruiting gossip that he frequented the 1-900 numbers. He also talked with Steve Figueroa, one-time AJC sports reporter who had good recruiting channels, and again—a nice guy, though he wouldn't deny allegations he was a Georgia Tech grad.

From the beginning, there were also boosters and "insiders" who were connected to the coaches. None of their names shall grace this exposition, but their tidbits were always available and always appreciated. They could tell you things, or at least say, "I don't know, but I can find out." At the very least, it was possible to discover which prospects would be visiting campus soon, and soon that scoop would be on Vin's page. "We hear Montego Powers will be on campus in July" might be the page's careful phrasing.

There was also the traditional investigative technique known as "taking Rodney to lunch." Coach Rodney Garner was the Man in Georgia recruiting, and—particularly in the early days—he didn't really mind spilling a few beans, as long as those beans were served with a nice lunch. Sometimes there would be a wealth of new information, and it was clear someone had taken Rodney to lunch.

Vin ran the Georgia recruiting page for two or three years, including his own crash of the Emory server system one Signing Day—a recurring theme and hallowed tradition for Georgia pages covering this subject. When it was time for him to move on, he handed the keys to the site to his friend Charly in Athens. This was around 1999.

It was Charly Pou who branded the site with the name we all remember, The Grapevine. He was a big fan of the Marvin Gaye and Credence Clearwater Revival versions of that song, and his page bore its title in bold letters, with "I heard it through the Grapevine" as its slogan.

Today, people tend to remember the Vent "in the days when it was the Grapevine," conflating the two pages. But they were actually different entities that shared a passion and a lot of the same users. Quite often, when the Vent would crash or be down for maintenance, Charly would receive anxious e-mails: "What did you do with the Vent?" "When's it coming back?" He'd explain he had nothing to do with any of that, but folks didn't really believe him. These Internet people were all in league, right?

They were also *certain* he knew where Jasper Sanks, or some other bigtime recruit, was going next February. Maybe he even had some say in the matter. He'd once again explain, "I don't know. I promise." A likely story. He was the *Grapevine*, dammit!

By 2000, the recruiting industry was taking on a more definite form, and the new, specialized site runners—people like Jamie Newberg, Steve Patterson, and Scott Kennedy—were developing their own reporting. But already the "hobbyist" days of the Internet were vanishing, and the dictum that "you can't sell stuff online, because information wants to be free" was fading. To various extents, tension lines were already forming around recruiting information and the audience it pulled.

At first, the Grapevine used the various devoted recruiting sites as Charly did with other sources, and it was all good. He always gave credit for the info and linked back to the site where he got it, paying back info with free advertising. It was a good tradeoff.

Charly published the 'Vine for five years before burning out, as happens to everyone involved in the business of recruiting high school kids (reporters, coaches, families, and the kids themselves).

At this point another Charlie entered the scene—Charlie Norris, known to Venters as redclayhound. A Sandersville true-red Dawg fan, Norris was a hardcore recruiting junkie from way back, the kind who still had his ancient, yellow press clippings and still pined after the kid Auburn got back in '67. He was and is loved by all who have known him.

By now, a circle of devotees was forming, one that became the nucleus of the early Vent moderators. It included names such as redclayhound, Groo, GaDawg, Steve Patterson, and Dawg C, another truly nice human being, as well as a vigilant mod who could do things on a computer that intimidated the Russians.

Groo was no techno-slouch, either, and he set up redclay's Grapevine in a new blog format. The idea was an easy, no-frills page whose operator could post on the fly. The URL was now georgiagrapevine.com.

Redclay did a terrific job with the page, his passion shining through with his fans, until he received word one day that the field of Georgia recruiting was getting a little crowded. More on that later.

The Grapevine was discontinued, having served the Georgia fans well for more than ten years.

It Came from Pluto

Meanwhile, college recruiting, from its humble beginnings, had become an Internet monster--though it started rather quietly.

As one example, Jamie Newberg worked for an Atlanta local TV show called *Countdown to Kickoff,* all about Southern recruiting. At the outset of the digital revolution, he helped to start a site called Border Wars simply to accompany his printed publication of that name. But again, the response outstripped all expectations. Quickly the electronic version overwhelmed the paper one. Soon Newberg was logging an astonishing 1.8 million page views on Signing Day.

By this time, the whole dot-com thing was in full bubble. A Seattle visionary named Jim Heckman[1] raised $80 million in venture capital to push his version of the idea forward, starting a national network known as Rivals.com.

Later, having sold his company to a Tennessee group, he also started a rival for Rivals: Scout.com. So yes, the same dude started the two big networks, Scout and Rivals.

Except Scout forced him out, then hired him back. Confused yet?

Me too. Maybe the best thing for you and me to do is to get back to Jason. Remember Jason? Back in '96?

Jason knew about the Grapevine and about the little group of Georgia sites then emerging. He wasn't going to write a blog, and he wasn't going to do the deep, daily grit-work of running down recruiting rumors.

Neither of these were his thing, and they were being done well by others anyway. He thought what was lacking was a good, thorough *informational* site. It could have rosters, schedules, and general miscellanea people might be interested in knowing. As

---

[1] I have no real insight on Jim Heckman. I just wanted to point out that I once had a friend named Jim Hellman. Heck, man!

multimedia became more possible, that could be added, too—in the late nineties, anything more than text, simple graphics, and the occasional blinking header made a page all but unloadable.

Really, however, the point of this exercise was for Jason to prove he could create a site. It was the act of an intrigued hobbyist—but with vast, unintended and mostly wonderful consequences.

At Jason's office was a system of servers named after planets. "Pluto," like its namesake (still a proud and highly esteemed planet at the time) was "way out there" in the scheme of these servers. So Jason's new project was known as the Pluto Page.

He uploaded his content, via HTML 1.0, plain vanilla and easy to design, and somehow people began finding their way there. Again, you are reminded that this was pre-Google, which was incorporated two years later, in 1998. Searching for subjects of interest was as much an art as a science in those days. "Keyword searching" and other techniques were in their infancy.

You could enter "Georgia Bulldogs" into Yahoo or WebCrawler or AltaVista and wade through page after page of links, many of them about the Eurasian country of Georgia or how to care for a bulldog—again, library pages scattered on a floor. But people were crawling on their hands and knees on that floor, they were making it to Pluto, and the audience was growing.

"What's in it for these people?" That's what Jason had to ask himself at this point. "If I'm a Dawg fan, I'll come once, look over everything, and come back—exactly why?" How to make those visitors into frequenters, that was the question.

What his site lacked was a solid hook. Who, exactly, were these mysterious visitors whose presence registered only as "page views"?

He researched the concept of *signatures*—a way for a visitor to say, "Hey, I was here." In other words, most of the Web was about providing content, but what made the Internet different was *interactivity*. Sure, you could yell at your TV screen and throw a beer can at it. But the little head coach inside the screen didn't duck. He had no idea you felt the way you did. On the Internet, you could step up, have your say, and leave a footprint.

So, Jason thought—what if we allowed the guests to provide the content themselves? Clearly that would be a game changer.

He didn't know it, but he had taken a giant step toward the virtual beer-can-throwing that would become known as the Vent.

The earliest form of "signatures" or interactivity on the Web was something now considered quaint in web design circles: the "guest log," where people could leave their names just as they did in a visitors' book.

Jason provided an area for the readers to say a word, perhaps a sentence, and it quickly took on a life of its own. The visitors began to talk not just to the site, but . . . among *themselves*. One small step for Jason, one giant leap for fankind.

Suddenly a static Web page, a repository of rosters and schedules, became the world's virtualest electronic cocktail party, a very real, virtual dialogue—and to try it was to like it. Georgia football fans had a new passion, just about the time the program itself wasn't much to be passionate about.

Servers and Signatures

For the sake of history, it should be noted that the Vent wasn't the first discussion forum for Georgia football. In the early days, America Online, Prodigy, and Compuserve were the most common "training wheels" for learning to ride the new vehicle known as the Web, and these systems offered a bit more sophistication, including discussion forums.

The Prodigy service, founded way back in 1984, had a lively Georgia Bulldog section, and a small cluster of its online yakkers later became regulars on the Dawgvent. America Online (1991) had a very quiet and inactive folder for Bulldog discussion.

Basically, if you weren't on Prodigy, you had no real place to talk about the red and black online.

Visiting the Internet Archive's "Wayback Machine" reminds those of us who were around just how different the Internet was in those days. Multimedia was mostly impractical. First-gen html code was primitive, so pages took a great amount of work to update.

One of the biggest differences was that on the Internet, *nobody bought anything.* If anyone on a Prodigy or America Online board tried to sell you something, he was quickly and roundly condemned—the Internet belonged to the people, and it wasn't to be monetized. As a matter of fact, people believed it would never happen. In a classic bit of Newsweek prophecy of 1995, about why the Internet was doomed to fail, the author wrote:

> *Then there's cyberbusiness. We're promised instant catalog shopping—just point and click for great deals. We'll order airline tickets over the network, make restaurant reservations and negotiate sales contracts. Stores will become obsolete. So how come my local mall does more business in an afternoon than the entire Internet handles in a month?*

I know, right?

Later, the author observed, "A network chat line is a limp substitute for meeting friends over coffee."

He never came out and said, "You kids get off my lawn!" but he would have been surprised by the "chat lines" to come and the global economic power of Amazon.com.

In the nineties, the Atlanta Journal-Constitution had a popular feature called the Vent. It had this same goal of giving readers a "signature," a way to get in on the act. Readers sent in one-line "vents" about bad traffic spots or rude cashiers or poor plays by the Braves' shortstop. *Venting.*

It seemed to Jason that what he had was a digital "Vent," a place where Georgia fans could share their two cents' worth, while keeping the two cents in their pockets. Another reality: In '96, the year of the Vent's inception, the Georgia Bulldogs were nobody's idea of a football dynasty. It was Jim Donnan's first year as head coach, as well as the last year the team didn't attend a bowl. So if you wanted to talk about Georgia football, basically you were going to vent.

Losing at home to Southern Miss to start the season? Who didn't have a verbal brickbat for that one? Losing by 40 to Steve Spurrier in Jacksonville? Now you could express your emotions over that without having to take on the persona of "Rufus from Snellville" on the call-in show.

Twenty years later, the forum might have been given a different name, one that didn't brand it as a gripe-fest. But it's the Dawgvent now, henceforth, and forever.

In these early days, people were posting on the Dawgvent as they did on the AJC Vent: in one-line shots, a little more like today's Twitter. Quickly that grew old; "guest log" technology wasn't cutting it. But Jason (DM, DawgMaster, on his board) was on the job, and soon he found CGI-scripted (Common Gateway Interface) message board code that was publicly available as a resource for Internet forums. Long-form statements were now a possibility.

This caused some excitement: paragraphs replaced sentences. Imagine being confined to one sentence to describe your day when you came home from work—then, after months of this, being told you could say as much as you wanted. Now you could vent and vent some more about the defensive stylings of Joe Kines, or whether that Bobo kid would ever muscle up his noodle arm.

Remember, all this activity was transpiring on a server on the office network of Jason Brooks. He hosted a fabulous, wide-ranging conversation among people from all over the world who were Georgia Bulldog fans, all in a little box in the back of his workplace. It was his baby, that baby was growing out of its crib, and it was time to move.

This is where the "Centurion" part of the obscure "pluto-centurion," known to Vent-lore aficionados, comes from. The friend ran a business called Centurion Systems, and he offered to host the server on his network. Pluto.centurionsys.com became the address of the Dawgvent. The friend was glad to do it, since it seemed like a small favor.

He had no idea what other-worldly forces he had unleashed.

DawgVent

- Who wants to see ... - **Herschel's Ghost** *20:13:50 4/15/97* (0 Responses)
- Atco Dawg--Baseball........................ - **HawkDawg** *20:09:15 4/15/97* (0 Responses)
- erratic behavior indicative of bobo's problems - **barnesville dawg** *18:59:01 4/15/97* (0 Responses)
- GA vs USC - **JD** *18:13:08 4/15/97* (0 Responses)
- I've learned my lesson and ... - **DAWGbabe** *18:09:55 4/15/97* (5 Responses Latest)
- Techbert- Remember the Tech player who got in a bar fight... - **South GA Dawg** *18:04:37 4/15/97* (1 Respo
- Two Questions About The Fight - **Techbert** *15:40:30 4/15/97* (15 Responses Latest)
- Update on UGA Spring Football - **George P. Burdell** *14:04:43 4/15/97* (3 Responses Latest)
- PLEASE HELP? NORTH SOUTH GAME - **TOPDAWG** *13:32:27 4/15/97* (1 Responses Latest)
- Fights - **Georgia Gal** *13:02:10 4/15/97* (3 Responses Latest)
- At Least. - **StudentDawg** *12:24:12 4/15/97* (0 Responses)
- On the better side of UGA athletics - **BIOCHEMDAWG** *11:19:59 4/15/97* (3 Responses Latest)
- Tell me why 98 will be better than 97 - **boroDawg** *11:18:23 4/15/97* (2 Responses Latest)
- Excuse the Idiot posting as Upstatecock, he is actually at the citadel. - **'CockPit™** *11:10:11 4/15/97* (3 Resp
- Fellow Venters, have I ever let you down? (article in the R&B about Bobo and Tolbert) - **BIOCHEMDAW(**
- Tech throws 250 large at B.Davis? - **uga88** *10:59:21 4/15/97* (14 Responses Latest)

Dawgvent, April 15,1997

Birth of a (Dawg)Nation

By 1998, the year the recruiting sites really took off, Vent traffic was overwhelming the Centurion system. National Signing Day of that year was almost apocalyptic. Servers simply didn't have much capacity in those days; they responded to high traffic by going on the fritz. At Jason's office, the system surrendered to an avalanche of users frantic to know who signed Jesse Miller, Terrence Edwards, Boss Bailey, and Nate Hybl.

At Centurion Systems—what fresh hell was this? Nobody was pleased by the systems crash—"You're telling me *what,* Brooks? We were shut down by a FOOTBALL DISCUSSION?"— but the fans weren't exactly pleased, either. You'd run to the home computer for your desperate, Signing Day Vent fix, and instead you'd get an error page ("HTTP 404" FILE CANNOT BE FRIGGIN' FOUND").

On this of all days? It was the UGA fan's equivalent of Santa being stuck midway down the chimney.

Jason was getting it from both ends, co-worker and fan alike. Maybe, he observed ruefully, it was time to shut the doors to the site. He actually considered that. He had a life, a wife, and a job, plus a regular gig playing lead guitar for a Blue Man Group tribute band[2] and life was becoming more demanding.

On reflection, he realized the Vent deserved better than to be put down like a stray dawg, so he began to seek donations— what we'd now call "crowdsourcing," though, again, that terminology had yet to be coined.

For Jason, this was the most dramatic moment of the whole saga. He was used to user "handles" and their brief comments. People were often thought of in the Internet community as "fonts." But here were letters on real paper, from

---

[2] All right, that last part isn't true. But if it had been, how funny would that be?

real people, from across the country, and as he opened them, checks and currency fell out. Many came with notes that said, "I don't post, but the Dawgvent is the best thing about the whole Internet. There's no other place for me to get this information about my Dawgs. Please keep it going, and if this isn't enough, I can send more."

The pluto.centurionsys.com days were over nonetheless, but now Jason knew the Vent had taken on a life of its own. He would build a new home for his site—and he could ditch the clunky "Pluto.centurion.sys" address, which wasn't exactly catchy. It was time to buy a domain just for the Vent.

Jason and his wife were on their way out of town for a little vacation. His wife was going through the stack of mail she'd grabbed on her way out the door. Looking through the letters and the checks, she marveled at the distance many of them had traveled—fans on the West Coast or at an army base in Germany; an international businessman in Rio; people from all over, communing on a little server in somebody's office.

"These people are from everywhere. Not just around here," she said, as their car moved down the freeway. "You have to call your new domain the Dawgnation."

Over time the name *Dawgnation* stuck, not just around the Vent but elsewhere. Others laid claimed to the natural branding of the label, but the true origin was the Jasonmobile on its way out of town. It became possible for the Grapevine to be hosted on Jason's new server.

Another new member of the family was the Anti-Orange Page, cartoonist and humorist Amy Moore Brown's gathering for everyone who hated teams wearing orange. (Motto, "Rednecks turn orange in the fall.") It was a small world. Those who ran these sites tended to be in their twenties, tech-savvy, and familiar with each other.

Things proceeded smoothly for a good while. The Vent continued to reach new users, but in a way, football itself changed. Seasons no longer observed the tight bookends of Fall Camp and bowl season. The conversations just kept going, twelve months a year, seven days a week. Some online fans made arrangements to meet and became true friends. Others made arrangements to meet behind the Majik Mart off Route 6, roll up their sleeves, and solve their differences. Your greatest friends and your sworn enemies were all there on the Dawgvent.

The Vent developed its own lingo. For instance, in the early days there were "Beans" and "Bashers." From the former, like good, bland butterbeans, never was heard a discouraging word. They loved the coach, whoever he was at the time, and would countenance no ill words about him. Perhaps the most quoted Bean line, by an eternally sunny poster known as Bassndawg, was that 1999 defensive coordinator Kevin Ramsey, he of the backwards cap and the Auburn humiliation, was "the greatest defensive mind in college football."

"Bashers," on the other hand, never seemed to love the coach or more than one or two of the players. Their own name for their tribe, however, was Realists. If you were *smokin' angry* most of the time, and you were certain in the depths of your soul that next season would be just as much of an abomination as the present one—Son, you were a *realist*. Football's a bitch and then you die.

The poster Jedi Master devised a helpful diagnostic scale measuring posters from 1 (Full-on raging, teeth-gnashing Basher), to 10 (Hopeless, drooling Bean). He established a matching poster for each number from one to ten. Everybody argued about their score. In later years, "Beans" became "Disney Dawgs," with a nod to the land of happily-ever-after supposedly inhabited by their football outlooks.

As the community developed its own culture, new visitors to the Vent had to learn the lingo of the moment, figure out the resident characters, and assimilate the local customs, much like moving to Guam or parts of lower Alabama. But it was worth it for a rollicking, 365-day-per-year gabfest about the greatest of all life topics, the Georgia Gol' Dang Bulldogs. It was like sitting over the checkerboard in front of Floyd's barbershop, with Goober, Barney, Opie, and several thousand of your buddies, all with the last name of Dawg. Or let's just call it the world's largest tailgate.

When you surfed over to the Vent, your eyes were immediately gladdened by those red lines of type, always with fresh viewpoints and controversy. In the early days, you saw a green privet hedge border—just like in Sanford. The simple border alone was a beloved element, illustrating the passionate love people had for Venting in the late nineties.

Alliances and Rivals

By 1999, it was happening again. The site traffic was too big for its latest britches. Jason had created a red-and-black Frankenstein, an electronic monster that just kept growing and ripping through its fresh togs from Bubba's Big and Tall Shop. Not only was the traffic almost as bad as the physical variety after a game, but admin duties were consuming more and more of Jason's time, impacting his work and family life.

He had to admit the truth. This was no longer something he could do alone. But he had a Hewlett-Packard buddy named Steve Patterson, a nice guy and Dawg fan, and Jason now approached him as a potential partner.

This joining of forces was mirrored by the trend of other sports sites, all of them outgrowing their hobby-launched creators. Most of the more prominent fan bases had discussion sites, and networks were being formed to take in the sites of as many collegiate programs as possible.

The Vent became part of the AllianceSports network, which concentrated on the Southeast. But the dot-com era was boom-and-bust: Alliance, in turn, was acquired by Rivals.com in 2000. Rivals, in turn, went bankrupt, and the Alliance owners bought the remaining assets back for pennies on the dollar.

When Rivals was relaunched, so was the Dawgvent under the UGASports.com brand and domain. By now, they had it all figured out, and when Yahoo acquired Rivals in 2007, the company paid a reported 100 million dollars.

Steve Patterson, once known simply as Oregon Dawg, had been in the U. S. Infantry before earning a degree at Oregon State. He was looking for some exciting way to grow professionally, and in the fan site business he found it.

For nearly sixteen years, Steve *was* the Dawgvent for tens of thousands of users. Through his guidance, the site grew from a simple discussion forum to a journalistic voice—and a steady business—in the world of sports. A lover of photography, he began publishing practice photos and even snippets of film. He introduced a popular podcast. Steve understood that with the Internet, there were virtually no limits to what could be done.

Jason faded into the backdrop to a certain extent. After a while, he might make a brief appearance in a conversation, and most users failed to realize he was their cyber-grandaddy. He watched as UGASports.com reached new heights and became truly profitable as a part of the Yahoo network. Jason summarizes his experience: "It was never about the money. In the end I have a good story, some memories, and a number of life-long friends."

It was Steve who shepherded the site through that period when pay-for-content was introduced. Naturally, this would be a controversial development in the age of Napster and the stubborn demand that "information wants to be free."

Steve helped sell readers on the idea that a few bucks per month allowed them to have full-time reporters, advanced recruiting information, and various bells and whistles that simply couldn't be provided without the users pitching in. Everyone would remember the "good old days" of casual Venting on a site that just might crash if the discussion became too popular. But it's also true that people enjoy paying for something that provides value, and they're in no way opposed to being thought of as "insiders."

For a small subscription fee, they could hear the gossip on that running back from over in Whatsit.

They could be insiders, everyone his own Joe Terranova.[3]

The Dawgvent, June 20, 2000

---

[3] Terranova means, literally, "new world," which college football recruiting became. Tom Lemming's name, on the other hand, means "small rodent known for jumping off cliffs in packs," which more than a few users of these sites became.

Cyber-Therapy

But what really made the "pay Vent" go was the decision to split the forum two ways. The old Vent had developed such broad-ranging conversation that true sports devotees were becoming impatient. "Take it to the Water Cooler," they would impatiently reply to off-topic remarks. They were referring to a board where politics, religion, and other controversies could be broached.

After all, for days on end—particularly during the offseason, but not always—people would discuss everything but football. During one era, for some reason, Venters would post single lines from songs. At first, it was a "guess the song" thing, but since everybody knows a song or two, the Vent would be completely overrun by lines from songs for days at a time.

Or arguments would break out over whether Corona was a true beer, what should happen to President Clinton, or even (gasp) the volatile issues of race or religion. People would bang futilely on their keyboards, all but weeping: "Take it to the Water Cooler!" But nobody really did. Most didn't even know where to find the "Water Cooler," and besides, it took an extra click—a click that could be invested on checking out the "eye candy" in somebody's post, once "sigs" (recurring JPEGs or favorite quotes) could be appended to posts. Once you were on the Vent, you weren't about to leave the room and miss who-knew-what.

Steve could have laid down the law, sports only, but he also knew there were some very strange and slightly scary people on the Vent. Instead, he left the board right where it was and how it was—and made a new place for the football-only group. Which, happily, was something that could be monetized.

Anything and everything, within decent bounds, was fair game on what was now known as the "Free Vent." But now there was the "Pay Vent." It would be a premium board, dedicated to sports and sports only (or, as we say in Georgia, "football and football only").

Those fed up with discussions of beer and dating conquests were all too ready to fork out subscription money. Think of it: a place better than this world; a place about all football, all the time; a place where nobody posted song lyrics; the hope of an eternal posting life, protected by the Golden (Pay) Gate.

Soon the name of the free board was changed to The Chat, or Dawg Chat. Over time, the two boards, the Dawgvent (on the pay side) and the Chat (free) became entirely different environments with their own populations, and even a little friction between them.

Some, in misty-eyed nostalgic, bemoan the day when "it became about money." They miss the free-wheeling era when the sports junkies and the just-here-for-gab crowds mingled as one. (Also, that was back before my arthritis flare-up, and when our Clarence was just a young-un, and gas was—well, they paid *you* to take it.) The nostalgia loses sight of the fact that this was an inevitable stage of board evolution, much like the day the first human decided to stop being a fish, tracked water out of the pond, and built himself a football stadium.

September 11, 2001 was a notable date in Vent history, just as it was for the USA. Those who were Venters experienced the shock of the terror attack together, an experience of virtual community that no one would ever forget. In a way, this was a day when Venters realized the power of the new medium of Internet society.

People found they could share genuine emotions, both positive and negative, in a way they might not in other places. In the beginning of the morning, people were discussing the new Georgia coach, Mark Richt, who had just lost to South Carolina in his first SEC game. The Houston Cougars were coming on Saturday. Already the new coach was being questioned.

Then came the first post of the rest of our lives, along the lines of, "Is anyone watching the news?"

A plane had hit a World Trade Center building in New York City. How could such a thing happen? A few theories were thrown out.

Then, just a while later, someone else posted that it had happened to *another* building in the WTC.

America was under attack.

On the only comparable occasions, such as Pearl Harbor or the JFK assassination, there had been nothing like the Internet. It had been more of a front-porch world then. You called your loved ones on the phone, huddled with neighbors, gathered in your children.

But with this event, the personal experience was something as new as the idea of a domestic terror attack—dozens of people, faceless fonts but caring ones, commiserating and theorizing together; people uplifting other people whom they might never meet in person; a futuristic comfort for a futuristic terror.

Over the next few days and weeks, football was forgotten, the Houston game was rescheduled for December, and Venters came together at all hours to work through the new geopolitical realities together. As a matter of fact, since the team already had a BYE after the scheduled Houston game, there was a very rare two-week blank in the football schedule. So while the game faded to a backdrop, people continued to show up at the Vent, keeping up with the newest information on the attack.

On September 13, this reporter sat down to write a short poem for the board. It was called "The Binch," it was a reworking of "How the Grinch Stole Christmas," and for me it was nothing more than a way to deal with my shock and awe in a creative way. But a remarkable thing happened. At least one Venter shared the poem by e-mail, and that person shared it. Then the next one . . .

Within twenty-four hours, "The Binch" had traveled around the world, eventually being called by one magazine "the most forwarded e-mail of all time," and for a number of days it shut down my life (and the work of a publishing house; people Googled my name, found the house, and were trying to contact me through my publisher). The little ditty became a small phenomenon in itself, a tiny footnote to a historic event. The work of the Vent reached as far as the *New Yorker* magazine and Ground Zero itself—from where one of the searchers told me the poem was pasted up everywhere as an encouragement. New York's ABC News did a segment in which children of all colors each recited a line from "The Binch," and thousands of radio stations read the poem. All of that started on the Vent.

The obsession for football created the board. But people, with all their diversity and idiosyncrasies, made the board into something far more unique and fascinating.

Welcome to the Big Top

Once the Vent had hit its stride, users often mentioned how addictive the site was. Spouses felt cheated upon ("It's me or that computer! Choose!"). Vacationers panicked—no modems on the campground! We'll miss something!

If you fell into a coma for a week, you were liable to need the Vent decoder ring when you woke up. What does this BOAISY thing stand for? [4] Why do people keep saying, "More and more it's Andy McCollum?" [5] What name is Paintdawg/Rolo/Wu hiding under this week? What's a "tickle pile"? [6] What the heck is "Cawgs or Gie?" [7] Why am I being told to "bake ham" for Ron Zook? [8]

And of course, the perennial question, carried on from fathers to sons, across generations—what does "Germans" mean? Problem was, it was too hard to explain. But heck, man, let's try.

There's a line in the film *Animal House*: "Was it over when the Germans bombed Pearl Harbor?" Sure, it was the Japanese, for gosh sake, but Belushi's character didn't know that.

---

[4] "Bend Over And I'll Show You." Look, it wasn't my idea.

[5] During the search for Richt's replacement, someone wanted Paul Johnson to be hired. He kept insisting, "More and more it's (likely to be) Paul Johnson." But Andy McCollum, then Middle Tennessee State's head coach, was an even more unlikely choice. Perhaps because it was funnier, "Andy McCollum" replaced Georgia Southern's Johnson in the catch phrase. For years, I wondered if I remembered this wrong, but several Venters from that era confirm their memories that it was Johnson originally.

[6] A form of on-campus recreation for Georgia Tech students, first suggested in an extremely offensive 1999 Saxondawg post that, alas, is lost in the dust of time.

[7] The late poster known as Ghost had some spelling challenges, particularly at specific times, but there was nothing inconsistent about his passion for Georgia football.

[8] "Bake ham" is what we do in the South when someone dies or loses his job as head coach at Florida.

Back to the Vent. On virtually every single page of the site, someone shares news that everyone's already heard. Welcome to last week, dummy! Massive shaming ensues.

Sometimes it's ancient news—if so, it probably comes from the legendary poster known as "Dr. Scoop." Early in Vent history, merchants of stale information were punished with headline-style phrases such as, "First-Time Dad Adam Reveals: It's a Boy!" or "Attila the Hun Invades Puberty."

At some point, of course, someone's headline was, "Japanese Bomb Pearl Harbor." To which some Belushi devotee wryly corrected it as, "Germans!"

Followed by a barrage of abuse until it was discovered this was an *Animal House* reference. Soon people began using "Germans Bomb Pearl Harbor" and then, finally, the shorthand: "Germans!" Every time, of course, the whole thing, including Japanese vs. Germans, had to be reexplained to newcomers.[9]

Newbies, of course, must be shamed. It's a rite of passage. If you don't want people to know you're a rookie, don't ask what Germans means. Or who Astrodawg was.[10] And God help you if you ask "what the black bones are for" or "what time is the Dawg walk?"

---

[9] Some have questioned the idea that the Vent initiated the "Germans" meme. While it can't be proven either way, the best evidence indicates that indeed it started with the Dawgvent. The evolution of the phrase is simply too convoluted to have happened simultaneously on various boards; the Vent was a particularly early forum; and the Vent was public, so that rival fans could read it and begin using it on their own boards.

[10] Astrodawg was a purported "insider" known for his long, after-dinner walks with Coach Donnan. Like all such posers, his practice reports and scoops always turned out to be, in the phrasings of today, "a big nothing sandwich."

Venters hate lots of folks—our shared resentments bond us as one big, hatin' family—but whom do we love? Two categories. 1) Second-string quarterbacks, and 2) "Insiders." The latter, of course, *know* things. They fraternize with those gods who inhabit the Butts-Mehre building, if only in the mailroom, or they've wangled a chance to peek at a practice.

Every Vent generation seems to have its insiders, some of them actually legit. Among the first of these was an executive who posted frequently on the board and was also close to the teams. He posted some of the first practice reports under the handle of Bulldog Bud (not to be confused with Bulldog Bob, currently on the Insider Pantheon). Though Bud was close to certain coaches, those coaches never figured out his identity, and it drove them crazy. They stalked the perimeter during practice, eyeing everyone with suspicion, but Bulldog Bud's secret identity was never cracked.

The greater appeal of the Vent, of course, is that *everyone's* an insider of sorts if he or she is loyal enough to keep reading and to learn the lingo. Someone throws in a "hey, twirl" [11] and you smile knowingly, feeling just a bit superior when newer posters ask what it means. If you were around way back in 1998, and could tell your children and grandchildren about the Great Orange Purge, [12]

---

[11] Twirl Dawg was not only a Venter but one of the baton twirlers on game day. Naturally, she was a popular poster so that countless posts began, "Hey, Twirl..."

[12] In the days when the Vent was a free board, UT Vol fans were the greatest of nuisances—utterly obnoxious during their team's very brief era of greatness. One night, in a digital blitzkrieg, the Vent moderators vacated the membership logs of all posters bearing the wording "Vol" or "Orange" or "UT" or "Smokey" or "ElvisInOKC" in their names. That last one requires a footnote, but I don't know how to do that from inside a footnote. Sorry.

then you knew what it must feel like to recount your memories from hitting the beaches at Normandy during the Big One.

So the Vent had its own big eVents, its oyster-roast meetups, its own special lingo, its own codes of conduct, and its own traditions. It had a "day crew" who kept banker's hours in their gab, and an almost wholly different "night crew," and the Vent would change its whole personality as Happy Hour became Cocktail Hour. But at any time of day, what counted most was its special cast of all-stars.

I thought long and hard about how to handle this part. There's simply no way to do justice to the vast number of characters who have shuffled across the virtual Vent stage and performed their magic. A few names, you'll notice, have trickled in here and there, but it's like an Oscar acceptance speech. You're going to leave somebody out, so it's best to err on the side of brevity.

There are, of course, what we've come in later Internet years to call "trolls"—online fight-pickers. There never has been, nor ever will be, a period when the Vent (or any other forum) is without its trolls. It's just part of the Internet experience. In highway traffic or forum traffic, you hide behind a wheel or a handle; you can be whomever you feel like being at the moment. The fact is, for many folks, Vent agitators play the part of the villain from downtown Wide World o' Rasslin'. It's a circus, not a salon for philosophers. Flame wars ensue, somebody gets "nuked" (only to be reincarnated under another handle), and Vent life goes on.

The forum also has its good guys—the unsung posters who are less confrontive by nature, and get along with the whole crowd. They tend to support the coaches, the players, the disappointing seasons, but mostly each other. Never flashy, these folks are rarely mentioned on "favorite Vent poster" lists, but they're the heart and soul of the Vent.

DV: The Next Generation

Just before 9/11, a poster named Radi Nabulsi joined the site. His first memory of the Dawgvent is that of posters sharing urgent news updates from across the country. Radi was working as a photographer for the UGA Athletic Association, and he had become friends with fellow camera ace Steve Patterson.

As the Vent kept on going and growing, Steve hired Radi in 2007 to help run the site and grow the subscriber base. Radi, with his sense of humor and easy congeniality, caught on quickly with that base, and soon he was a fixture. After only a month, Steve asked him to take over day-to-day operations—just as Jason had once asked of Steve himself. Running the Vent is consuming work, and if you doubt that, ask the wives.

Though the growth continued, tough times arrived for the economy. Radi was asked to discharge a writer due to shrinking profits. Instead, Radi imposed on himself a sizeable pay cut in order to keep everyone on the payroll. He wanted the team to know that he believed in them that much.

Indeed it was an impressive team. ESPN was wanting to get into this fan site game, and the "Worldwide Leader in Sports" was recruiting lead reporter Anthony Dasher, recruiting specialist Kipp Adams, and Radi himself to help them build a Georgia site. Talks went on for months, hot and cold, until finally, just prior to the 2013 season, ESPN settled on hiring Kipp and Radi. They migrated over to the ESPN site network. Eric Winter, head of Rivals, said goodbye to the pair, but promised to keep in touch—which he did.

The "Worldwide Leader's" endeavor never quite took off, and Kipp and Radi ultimately left ESPN to pursue other opportunities. After a period writing for WXIA 11Alive in Atlanta, Radi was contacted by Winter, who had startling news. Steve had sold his rights to UGASports, and Rivals now wanted Radi back as the publisher.

This was a "dream job" opportunity for Radi. Having now worked for ESPN, Charter Sports, Sports Illustrated, and local Atlanta television, he had a strong enough résumé to find plenty of good media jobs, but his heart was with the Vent. He knew there was nothing else quite like it; nothing else so perfect for someone who enjoyed constant interaction with the fans.

"It's a family," he says. "We laugh with each other, we cry with each other, we fight like brothers and sisters and estranged uncles at Thanksgiving. Sometimes our familiarity finds the tender spots in each other, but in the end we all want the same thing: timely information, accuracy, and like-minded friends to talk to."

In just a few years, an obscure "Pluto board," created as a hobby for posting fun facts about a team, had become a large company, employing an impressive team. The same local newspapers who sneered at the Internet with its "fringe whackos" now scrambled to keep up with an onslaught of video, photography, interviews, up-to-one-second-ago recruiting rumors, and above all customer satisfaction that traditional media couldn't hope to duplicate.

A decade back, the old sportswriters had ridiculed them; now they were submitting their résumés to them.

Newsweek had written, upon declaring the inevitable failure of the Net, "What's missing from this electronic wonderland? Human contact. Discount the fawning techno-burble about virtual communities. Computers and networks isolate us from one another." [13]

---

[13] Clifford Stoll, "Why the Web Won't Be Nirvana," *Newsweek*, http://www.newsweek.com/clifford-stoll-why-web-wont-be-nirvana-185306; (February 26, 1995).

The writer had it exactly backwards. Or at least that's what many of us decided. At one time, I read the local paper religiously. The time came when I let my subscription lapse. The sportswriter was just a font, but Roe Dawg and Cartersville Dawg, Tee Dawg, Opie, Dawg C, JCarbo, and Groo—these were people I knew well, though I'd never met most of them in person, up to that point. Ironically, *Newsweek* went out of business a few years later. I read its obituary (wait for it) . . . on the Internet.

Radi says, "I've laughed so hard from behind this keyboard, and I've sobbed uncontrollably. I've raged. I've been soothed. And hopefully, when I die, the Powers that Be will leave

me logged in." Sounds like he likes the "human contact." Twenty thousand Venters would tend to agree.

Like Jason and Steve, Radi talks about the friends and the stories, the slightly weird world of online community. It's not really surprising that none of them mention the sports part. You come for the football, but you stay for the friendship.

If the Vent has taught us anything at all, there you have it.

Dawgerel: Ooga and Me

Doggerel is poetry that is irregular in rhythm and in rhyme, often deliberately for burlesque or comic effect. The word is derived from the Middle English dogerel, *probably a derivative of* dog.—Wikipedia

I found the Vent circa 1997. I'd been looking for a place to read about the Georgia Bulldogs on the Internet. I had accounts with Prodigy and America Online, but for some reason I never stumbled across the Dawgly discussion already established on Prodigy. When I saw the feeble Bulldog presence on AOL, I just figured Prodigy wouldn't be any better, so I missed the inception of the earliest fan group, one that carried over to Jason's board.

It was my older brother, a former Redcoat Band drummer (RC72Dawg), who asked me if I'd seen the new site where people talked Georgia football every day. I tried it and got sucked in within three seconds of Venting.

One day in 1998, a rumor spread like the latest social disease. According to "sources," Jim Donnan had gotten into a fistfight with his defensive coordinator, Kevin "Cool Breeze" Ramsey. As I thought about the whole thing, it became funnier and funnier within the arena of my warped imagination. I sat down and typed out a potboiler of a story, totally made up, about the confrontation, blow for blow and with dramatic, B-movie dialogue; a pulp fiction parody of the confrontation between our head coach and a raging younger assistant.

In my version, Jim Donnan was a two-fisted hero, fighting for goodness, manhood, and zone pass coverage. I chronicled their trash talk and eventual smack-down, blow for blow, rasslin' hold for hold. Eventually, the global adventurer Vince Dooley, away as usual on a cruise and Indiana Jonesish archaeological escapade, jetted in to break up the fight like a true he-man, with his faithful and lethal man-servant Erk by his side.

The response was quite a rush for me. YUGE page-views, and I experienced that phenomenon in which page views are your new cocaine. I'd written and drawn cartoons for magazines and even had collections of my cartoons published as books, but I'd never experienced *real time* feedback like this.

This was something more like standup comedy, where you improvised something on the spot and people laughed or didn't. If your act went over, you couldn't wait to get out on the stage again.

After that, I was among that crowd always looking for a way to get attention—in my case, through laughter (yes, there's Internet lingo for that, too: "attention whore." Sigh.)

One day, as the 1999 season was about to begin, I had one of those very strange inspirations, the kind a storyteller receives when his muse has had one too many at a muse bar. I thought, "I should write a game prediction for our Utah State opener, except I should write it in the Old Testament style of the King James Version."

Who thinks of something like that? I've always known my Bible pretty well. And the old King James style, with its thees, its thous, its beholds and its who-smiteth-whoms, seemed perfect for something as violent and patriarchal and near-reverential as college football. Just take out the Philistines and put in Gators, and you've got it.

So I began to write the battle prophecies of the hunkering hermit "Ooga." (What else could he be called? And what else would he do but hunker? See, this stuff writes itself.) After a short introduction, such as prophets always have in the ancient writings, Ooga began,

> *On the fifth day of the ninth month of the final year, there will come invaders from the west and the north, and they shall be the aggie-people of Oo-Tah! Like the locusts of Lithonia will they fall upon the ancient city of Athens, for are they not of the land of the lake of salt?*

Consider. If I'd ever had to submit this in person to a real human being, someone I had to look in the eye, I'd never have had the stones. I promise you that. It's too—plain old weird, right? But on the Internet, under a pseudonym, as the Tech nerd says, you can do that! One thing the Net has done has been to encourage the kind of spontaneous creativity that tends to be flushed out of editorial committees and traditional groupthink. You can take big risks and either fall on your face (only to have it quickly forgotten) or, just maybe, come up with something fresh.

I posted my first Ooga three minutes after thinking of it. Then I thought again: "Man, I'm going to have to change my handle. They'll think my ramp doesn't climb to the upper deck."

But of course, the returns came in rapidly, and they were surprisingly approving. Among the very first reactions was, "You've got to do this every week."

Sounded like a plan.

So for the next six years, that's what I did, though not consistently. I knew Ooga was a success the day I walked up to

Sanford Stadium, just before the Tennessee game in 2000, and saw a car with a huge banner that said, "Hickolian Hillbillies." As if *anyone* would catch the Ooga reference. I also saw several Ooga tee shirts in the crowd that day.

He Who Hunkers was fun to write, especially after I had used my cartooning background to render him visually. People seemed to look forward to each week's game prophecy, though he was, it must be admitted, worse than Mark Bradley in terms of prediction value. After all, the Dawgs were not only undefeated in his oracles, they invariably scrubbed their opponents from the face of the bloody, sodden earth, visiting equal wrath upon the friends and families of these opponents.

As a matter of fact, as each new game approached, it grew difficult for Ooga to devise a devastation more shocking and abysmal than what he had foretold the week before.

The readers didn't seem to care. As long as there were plenty of smitings and surplus gore and entrails, served with a healthy seasoning of "beholds" and "and los," the customer was satisfied.

It must also be admitted that some didn't get Ooga at all. Almost everyone missed the biblical origin, and folks seemed to think it was either Dungeons and Dragons language or I was aping *The Lord of the Rings*. Which would have made me a DragonCon Techie!

Some began to post about how they were sick of the whole thing. I wasn't offended. Ooga wasn't for everybody. Meanwhile, as the prophecies were passed around, others began to copy them— for example, an Auburn "cave man" rendition, though inappropriately using sixteenth century biblical form like Ooga's.

So after 2004, Ooga said, "And lo, my work here is done," and hung up his spiked club. To this day, some still ask what the hunkering hermit has to say about this or that, and he may or may not emerge from hiding to render a prophecy. But Saxondawg himself moved on to other forms of satire, as you'll see in this book.

This book includes a sampling of things I've written through the years, with a good bit of new material. I've added explanatory notes where needed.

You really wouldn't want to read *all* of Ooga's prophecies one after the other. Believe me on this. So I've included some notable ones, plus the major games of the 2002 season, and I've spaced them throughout the book, instead of clumping them together.

Like everyone else, I've felt my life to be enriched by the Dawgvent. For many years, as a lifelong Dawg fan who didn't attend the university, I actually didn't know too many people in the stadium when I attended games. The Internet introduced me to the new Georgia family I'd always craved.

My hope is that you'll get at least a tiny fraction of the joy from these pieces as I found in writing them, and that occasionally . . . you'll laugh like a Dawg.

Rob Suggs

Saxondawg
Preseason, 2017

Thanks for the Game Day Wedding!

1998

Dear [name]:

Heartfelt best wishes on your recent engagement to the love of your life!

I particularly want to congratulate you on your decision to be married at halftime, at midfield of Sanford Stadium.

And why do I assume the wedding is at halftime, at midfield of Sanford Stadium?

Easy! Because I noticed immediately that your wedding date matches a home game on the schedule of my beloved Georgia Bulldogs. After I saw this, and my wife brought me back to consciousness via smelling salts, I figured it out. You *had* to have a halftime football wedding in mind. It *had* to be at Sanford Stadium.

Otherwise, surely you'd never schedule your nuptials on this date. There are, as you know, *forty-six available Saturdays* that do *not* conflict with Georgia Bulldog home games. How hard would it be to pick one of those? You're smart enough, no question.

If you had an ordinary church wedding in mind, you—as an upright citizen and right-thinking American—would have quickly chosen one of *those—not* one of the only Six. Sacred. Holy days. Reserved for the attention to the love of *our* life.

All right, I'll admit, I did suspect you had taken leave of your senses entirely at first. I thought you truly intended to ask all your Bulldog friends—clearly the *best, most wonderful people on the face of the earth*—to choose between their God-gifted football game and your scripted, highly predictable, and *completely non-football-related* recitation of vows.

Then I told myself, "No! That cannot be! My friend [name] is simply manifesting [his/her] wicked, twisted sense of humor! And granted, it would be a highly offensive and tasteless attempt at a joke—but yes, it's true: the stress of wedding planning *can* cause bizarre behavior.

That's when it hit me. I grasped what was *really* up your sleeve. You chose Game Day because you wanted the 92,000 most wonderful people in the world, the only ones who count, at your wedding. Of course!

Consider the ingenuity of it: Every friend you have who is worth keeping is a Georgia Bulldog, and will, by definition, be pre-assembled in the same location. You need not give directions to some church or bowling alley—everyone can find Sanford Stadium.

Nor will you have to rent musicians and listen to somebody's cousin struggle through "You Are So Beautiful to Me" or "Love Shack." Because you'll have the Redcoats to play the Wedding March and the "Spell Marriage cheer."

(Give me a second. I said I wasn't going to cry . . .)

I myself will be happy to paint the banner for the bride and her dad to run through. The majorettes will make one lovely set of bridesmaids.

Allow me to suggest using defensive linemen for groomsmen, because their long arms will be best for batting down the cups thrown at you by some of the drunken visiting fans at your wedding. But think of the fun of having tens of thousands of people throw rice at you simultaneously.

Hey, and I can already hear Loran saying, "If anyone has objections, bark now or forever hold your peace."

I need to check the etiquette books for whether friends of the groom sit in the North Stands and the bride's in the South, or vice versa. Because I'm sure our ticket office will be happy to reroute all 92,000 people for that one occasion. Anything for you, right? Because you want a friggin' *Game Day* wedding. Inconveniencing people doesn't come into it, isn't that right?

My wonderful friend [name], I'm so glad you've chosen to do it this way. Because, confidentially, I've known so-called "fans" who are less loyal than you are, *who have actually scheduled their weddings during home games—away from the stadium!* In churches! In parks! In "destination locales" where you can't even see a TV during the vows!

Yes, you read that right. I'm told it's done all the time. Can you imagine anyone so obtuse, insensitive, unfeeling, and unDawgly, as to desecrate the high holy kickoff time with something as unfootball-like as a wedding ceremony?

Also, I know you'd never do that because you're aware of the obvious remedy you'd force your friends to pursue. That, of course, would be for us to follow you out of town in our RVs and have a massive tailgate outside your room during the honeymoon, guzzling our booze, singing our Dawg songs and playing our Larry tapes. Some of those are a *hoot* when paired with honeymoon action. ("I'm beggin' ya, Dawgs—hunker down one more time!")

Not that we'd do that to *you*—only those who'd commit a sick, sociopathic act of calendar cruelty against the red-and-black-clad loved ones who care about them. I'm so glad you know better.

By the way, which of the two kinds of fine china have you chosen: red or black?

Best wishes and Go Dawgs!

Saxondawg
Section 331
Aisle 16

Ooga Makes an Entrance

August 1999

Donnan's Dawgs were opening the season with Utah State. It was late summer, 1999. On the bulletin board known as The Vent, threads no longer stayed on page one for a day or two—they rolled off within hours. On August 31, a humble scribe in Chamblee, excited about the new season, decided to channel a game prophecy from Ooga, the Hunkering Hermit who foretells point spreads in the terminology of Old Testament warfare.

The scribe had his doubts—this was weird stuff. It might attract health care professionals rather than appreciative readers. But The Vent liked it. Maybe suggesting the need for greater numbers of health care professionals. At any rate, Ooga was an overnight star. In the beginning, you'll notice, he was "the

Hermit of Hahira," but the hometown ID was dropped for some reason. Here is his debut prophecy.

This is the Oracle of Ooga, the Hermit of Hahira, and these are his weekly prophecies as delivered unto Saxondawg, who is his messenger.

Hear, O dog-people! Ooga speaks! Heed ye the words of the hermit Ooga!

On the fifth day of the ninth month of the final year, there will come invaders from the west and the north, and they shall be the aggie-people of Oo-Tah! Like the locusts of Lithonia will they fall upon the ancient city of Athens, for are they not of the land of the lake of salt?

Hear Ooga, ye raiders! Ye savages of the land where the men have many wives and ride bicycles! Ye who would bow before graven images of Donnie and Marie, I say unto you: Gird up thy loins, warriors of Oo-Tah, and prepare to be ground like salt into the great lake of red!

Swift and sure shall be thy fate, yea, even minutes after the great Coin of Coweta has spun its course in the air and thy battle captains have taken the wind! Lo, verily, thy battalions shall take the wind and be blown away!

They shall weep and wail and offer lamentations, sniveling like unto their many cow-faced wives, that Quincy the Hurlsmith and Grant the Gruff would have mercy on them.

But hear me, O girly-men of Oo-Tah—mercy shall not be given! Yea, before the minutes have been thirty and the great marching musicians of the sweltering red coats have sounded your deathly dirge, you shall have been trampled!

With savage cries of blood-vengeance, the dog-warriors will have crushed your bones, and the great linebackers who dwell behind the Great Wall of Stroud shall cool themselves with draughts of thy blood in the southern heat.

Lo, and our cornerbacks shall wear thy scalps as trophies on their battle helmets, and thy blood will leave no unsightly stains, for our vestments, are they not scarlet?

Drawn ye shall be, and quartered, even unto thy assistant coaches and trainers. And the wallowsome whale-men of our offensive line will make necklaces of thy toes, and lo, these necklaces will be available unto the web pages of the athletic department, as fund-raisers.

Then paid ye shall be, thou mercenaries, paid unto the king of Oo-Tah the maker of schedules, for the privilege of going to war before the bloodthirsty hordes of Sanford! Paid in silver, paid in pieces of gold, but will thy blood-money cover the funeral costs of thy vanquished girl-warriors?

Nay! Run thee sniveling to thy appointment with Stephen F. Austin on the barren plains of Nacogdoches, for is he not just one man?

This is the Oracle of Ooga, and these are his prophecies! Ooga knows! Ooga also foretells Navy over Tech on a last minute field goal. Lo! Take the points!

The Curious Adventure of the Black Stripe

Long ago, in a galaxy far away, college football players threw on a jersey, strapped on a leather helmet, and went out to knock heads. The jerseys were plain—gray, black, or white, according to the evidence of early photography— with large block numbers. Maybe there was a stripe. Maybe not. Design principle was whatever went well with tube socks.

It didn't really make a difference. After a few flying-wedge kickoffs and single-wing scrums in a mud pit (all football was played in mud back in the day), you couldn't tell one team from the other anyway.

Most helmets looked like this.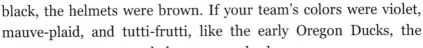

If your team's colors were red and black, the helmets were brown. If your team's colors were violet, mauve-plaid, and tutti-frutti, like the early Oregon Ducks, the helmets were also brown.

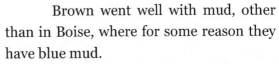

Brown went well with mud, other than in Boise, where for some reason they have blue mud.

Every now and then, a coach with a bold, visionary fashion sense came along and tried a newfangled concept such as this. But mostly, fans liked their football in no-frills, generic packaging.

One coach, fresh off the boat from

the Great War and the trenches of Verdun, attempted to import those Kaiser Wilhelm helmets with the single sharpened spike up-top, which would have enlivened those "flying wedge" plays.

But times were changing. The sport was developing a sense of style, haute couture, and that certain *je ne sais quois*. Or in Oregon, as they say, *je ne sais quack*.

Vince Dooley, though seldom mentioned in retrospectives of the fashions of Giorgio Armani, made a bold, *au courant* statement with *les Dawgs*. He modified the Bulldog helmet from silver to bright red, added a white stripe, and featured a pigskin-shaped G borrowed, with permission, from the house of Lombardi, then in vogue in the salons of Kenosha.

It was a full football makeover. All the guys on the team went to the barber shop for a fresh flat-top.

Several years later, a fan in Row 19 noticed the changes. "Is it just me or do we look different?" he asked. The rest of the section shrugged. Of course, in that time, people were still just learning to see in full color, as—again, according to the evidence of period photography—black-and-white was going out of style.

Things went along just fine for decades of Georgia football. Such innovations as sleeve stripes, no-sleeve-stripes, pant stripes, and no-pant-stripes were used without anyone particularly noticing. Meanwhile, your wife changed her hair, like totally, seventeen or eighteen times, and you never even looked up.

Our uniform pants went from silver to white to silver again. The shades of red in the jersey changed.

In the early 70s, the shades of some of the *players* even changed. It was all good.

Then Jim Donnan was hired. On his first day in office, he set up his coffee machine. He placed the family pictures on his desk, adjusted the drapes. Then he got on the phone, found the number of the equipment manager, and said, "Put a black stripe down the middle of the helmet."

As he said those words, crickets stopped chirping outside. In the next office, a secretary screamed. The sky grew dark.

Donnan could tell he had violated some long-sacred taboo. He grabbed the phone and called the equipment manager again, trying to take back the request. But it was too late. The ticket manager said, "Sorry, no take-backs. I'm afraid this black stripe will define you for as long as you're at Georgia. You'd better win big now. By the way, welcome to Georgia!"

The first season under the black stripe, Georgia was not invited to a bowl. Some blame the losing record, the awful defense—but the black stripe seems to have weighed on the host cities. After one look at the Dawgs, they said, "We can't submit our local fans to a bowl team that looks like that. Get me Kentucky on the line."

Leading advanced scholars of football theory now agree that the black stripe doomed the program to never-attained levels of so-so-ness.

"Those teams were packed with NFL talent—Hines Ward, Stroud and Seymour, guys like that," notes Dr. J. R. Heimlich, recent Nobel Prize winner in Quantum Football Schematics. "But that stripe! It breaks nine or ten rules of pigskin propriety."

In 2001, before the program could be shut down in shame, Mark Richt was hired. Among several impressive portions of his resumé, he came from an FSU program that was winning without a black helmet stripe. Immediately he was deluged with desperate pleas from fans. "Two things," wept the fans. "Number one: Remove that black stripe, for the love of everything holy. For God's sake, man—remove it! Number two: Win football games."

"Really?" replied the new head coach, who wore a haircut popularized during the leather helmet days and happened to like tube socks. "Okee dokee then. Here, pitch in. Could you carry this coffee machine?"

He picked up the phone, called the equipment manager, and did the deed. Birds began to sing. The stock market surged.

"Are you sure?" asked the equipment manager. "It's no take-backs."

"So I hear," said Richt. "But once I decide a thing, I do it. For example, I plan to run Jasper Sanks up the middle on the final play against Auburn this year."

"It's poor time management, but whatever," replied the equipment manager. "Long as you remove that damn hideous black stripe, you're gold."

Not everything went well that first season. Indeed, Georgia lost a heartbreaker to South Carolina in Richt's SEC debut. Steve Spurrier beat the Dawgs in his only Jacksonville matchup with Richt. Then, against Auburn, Richt, as good as his word, ran Jasper Sanks up the middle at the goal, and Georgia lost.

Even so, the crowd was strangely upbeat. On the way out of the stadium, they were heard chanting, "It's Great! To Have! No stripe on the HELmet, said, it's Great! To Have! No stripe on the HELmet . . ."

NOTES FROM AROUND THE SEC

2002

POTATO CHIP DISCOVERED BEARING LIKENESS OF "BEAR" BRYANT; PILGRIMS BEHOLD IN WONDER

MURKY CRICK, AL.—A Golden Flake potato chip bears the striking image of the late Coach Paul Bryant, according to area persons.

Amazing B'ar chip, before someone took a bite out of the ear and spoilt it for the rest of us.

Louella Mae Krimp, 37, an area natural wart remedy specialist, used the vending machine up at the local GrabbyMart. She was sharing the single-serving bag of Golden Flake with her coon dog Houndstooth when she discovered the remarkable apparition.

"It ain't the younger, slimmer B'ar, but the older, fatter B'ar," explained Ms. Krimp. "Daddy says these was the tater chips he plugged on his TV show, so it stands to reason he'd choose Golden Flake if'n he wanted to manifest hisself in a snack food. I checked in my Co-Cola bubbles, too but they was just Co-Cola bubbles, not the genuine tobacker spit of the B'ar or nothing."

The chip is currently on display under a Mason jar on Skeeter Rimshaw's checker board in front of the Western Auto hardware store, where it is drawing crowds of pilgrims who come to offer a moment of silent meditation with the potato chip, enjoy a Kodak moment, and whisper a reverent, "Roll Tide."

"Elroy Lee Tupman, they say he snuck himself a feel of the B'ar-chip and got the cure of his lumbago ailment. But I ain't letting people touch it," said Ms. Krimp. "Somebody already took a little bite out of the ear while I was away tinkling."

CLAUSEN ISSUES CHALLENGE TO THE ARMLESS

KNOXVILLE, TN—Tennessee quarterback Casey Clausen has been puzzled by the criticism.

All he said was that he could have beaten Georgia "'probably definitely with one arm by at least two touchdowns, maybe certainly or not.' I was misquoted. Sure I said it, maybe probably."

Now he has thrown down the gauntlet. "There's no doubt that I possibly may or may not take on all comers," Clausen said. "It's one hundred percent on, conceivably."

When asked about the rest of the team, Clausen said, "I'm told by our tutors there's no 'I' in Clausen, as far as anyone can tell, absolutely, no joke, maybe. So bring it on, I'll play with any armless or quadriplegic challenger, using only my good arm, or with one leg tied behind my back. I'm absolutely serious, possibly. Or maybe I'll use all my limbs, why not, ya know, could be, I guess not."

The spiky-topped quarterback with the trash-compacted face was quick to add, "My doctors won't clear me to do this, of course, but everyone should know I *would* win if they did clear me. By seven or eight touchdowns. It's a no-brainer—or just slightly a yes-brainer. I'm totally sure, pretty much, possibly. Feel me?"

GREENE AND SHOCKLEY MARRIED TO SAME WOMAN

ATHENS, GA—Quarterback is not the only position sophomore David Greene and freshman D. J. Shockley share, according to reports. Both are wed to the same woman.

"I dated them both in the spring, and I just couldn't decide who won the competition," said the area woman, who asked to remain anonymous. "David is more experienced and a better leader in the home, and he comes complete with Pollack—did you know they played on the same kids' team? Not everyone knows that. But D. J. is more mobile and has those intangibles."

The woman refused to comment on whether she rotated husbands based on day of the week, marriage situation, or whether she used some other system.

TOILET TISSUE IS AUBURN ISSUE

AUBURN, AL—Georgia has its mascot Uga and its "silver britches."

Mississippi State has cowbells.

And Florida has several old photographs of Steve Spurrier.

Now Auburn University seeks to make its own entry in the hall of storied college football traditions. Its symbol: the roll of toilet tissue.

"We roll Toomer's Corner after every win," says program supreme despot and area banker Bobby Lowder. "It's an Auburn thing. There's nothing so beautiful as Southern pines decked with rolls and rolls of double-ply extra-absorbent toilet paper."

Lowder adds, "It's a lovely sight to see all those drug store flashlights illuminating the various brands of tissue. The wife and I prefer the Charmin brand, which is squeezably soft, and available in baby blue, which may be one of our colors one day, next time we swap out all our traditions. But the common folk, they use the Dollar Store brand, and once you point a hose, all the tissues kind of shrivel together in all-in unity, and it's beautiful."

As athletic department officials explain, they'd like to make toilet tissue a worldwide reminder of "the loveliest village on the (jungle) plains." ("Jungle" is a recent branding attempt for Auburn's stadium. Given that the "War Eagle" program is actually about "Tigers," we can look forward to Auburn eventually covering the entire animal kingdom as well as all geographic forms.)

The Tiger Eagles have high ambitions for the household item. "Think about it," smiles alumnus Jethro "Cash Wad" Sistrunk. "How many times do people use toilet paper every day, all over the world? We want them to think of Auburn and all it means as they do their business with that tissue. We want them to hear our fight song during the flush, and see the Eagle circling the drain."

"LOU HOLTZ" MERELY A FRAT-BOY STUNT

COLUMBIA, SC—"The truth is, there never was a Lou Holtz," said South Carolina junior and mischievous frat boy Ernie Grope in a shocking statement last week.

The NCAA says it is investigating what it feels to be an unprecedented issue: the figurehead of a program who is literally a figurehead.

"It was all a stunt, and we're sort of tired of it," says Grope.

Grope and seven other students have confessed to propagating a long-running hoax involving a full-size wax puppet. The lifeless figure has been passed around from school to school for decades, as thousands of fans were duped into thinking the puppet was a real live, truism-spouting coach known to the world as "Lou Holtz."

Though only two thirds the size of a normal human, the figure is quite convincing.

"A few of us had hit the bottle a bit too much. We found an old Irene Ryan mask—"Granny" on *The Beverly Hillbillies*—and stuck the thing on this marionette. We were all laughing, then somebody had this brainstorm to have a ventriloquist stand next to the thing and make it say a lot of stale old clichés," explained Grope. "We called it 'Lou Holtz,' because it sounded like the 'loose bolts' that kept making the head fall off. We never thought anyone would take it seriously."

Grope continued, "It was just a harmless fraternity prank from our other chapters. Different guys stood by the puppet on the sidelines working the strings, posing as grad assistants. When the puppet would get fired, we'd just pass it on to the next school where our frat had a chapter—Minnesota, Notre Dame, Arkansas, whatever. Just having fun! Last thing we expected was for the dummy to win a national championship for the Irish in '88. Our apologies to #2 Miami. But you knew you let a dummy beat you."

When asked why the hoax has now been called off, Grope said, "Just moving on. Besides, 'Wooden Lou' has seen its better days. Portions of the face are kind of soggy and wrinkled up, as many have noticed. Big Bud, our ventriloquist, is drunk most of the time, spits a lot, and can't pronounce stuff. You've probably noticed that when 'Lou' speaks, too."

"During the Tennessee game," he said, "a wasp actually flew out of the dummy's eye socket, which horrified the cheerleaders. We figured we'd better call it quits before an arm fell off or something. Our last act is to have a duel between the puppet and Casey Clausen's bad arm on Pay-per-view."

When asked whether such a prank had ever been sustained so long, Grope said, "Have they found out about Paterno yet?"

Ooga vs. Clemson, 2002

You really don't want or need every single Ooga prophecy. Trust me on this, you don't. Instead, we're taking one memorable year, 2002, and scattering throughout the book the prophecies for the more important games—plus some of the Ooga "extras" from various times. We opened that 2002 SEC Championship season with Clemson at Sanford stadium.

Behold! These are the prophecies of Ooga, the wholly holy, highly hunky and hefty honky, the hunkering hermit of the heavenly hedges of Sacred Sanford, he who endureth yet again months of drudgery, of feeble girlygirl baseball, of accursedly wretched television reruns, with no recourse but to thinketh up h-words for his opening sentence.

And lo, doth not the offseason maketh the oracle ornery?

Doth not the months move forth as slow as the wit of the Chattering, Cheating Chair-Stackers of the Hickolian Hill People of Knoxville?

Doth not the off-season grate on the prophet's nerves like the giggling of the pen-pocketed peons of the Nattering Nimrods of NATS?

Doth not the glacial speed of the eight-month-wait anger the Hunkerer's blood like the prattling press conferences of the Zealous, Zig-Zagging Zookster of the Mulleted Minions of the Unspurritized?

But lo, good tidings of great joy! For even now, on winged footsies, the season approacheth, and Richt the Righteous coacheth, and the Defense encroacheth, and Van Gorder reproacheth.

And the People of the Dawg cometh forth belching flames, discarding forth the putrid pansies of past appetizer games, instead calling out, "Sendeth forth thy Clemson for a clash, as we clamor for a clobbering! Sendeth us the Dithering Doofus Danny Ford, for we kicketh not his hindquarters for several years, and we kind of misseth it!"

But above the trudging tumult of the tractors cometh a cry, that Danny Ford hath thrown his last cap, hath chewed his last chaw, and fumeth on the sidelines no more, but goeth forth to speak at lodge meetings and accept forth sappy plaques from women's groups.

So the People of the Dawg crieth out like a voice in the wilderness, saying, "Send forth a fitting warrior, worthy to lead the Clueless Clem Kadiddlehoppers of yore into bloody carnage!"

And the voice cometh back yet again, saying, "Shore thing, We sendeth a fresh young Bowden with nice hair and a nice diddy. Just don't taketh our cows, and leaveth us our farm equipment."

And the People of the Dawg snorteth in contempt, and spitteth a big loogie, and it floodeth, yea, the whole Anderson area, even unto the Piedmont, even unto suburban Greenville.

For the Clueless Clem Kadiddlehoppers, have they not become a feeble race, wimpish and unmanly as befitteth ACC she-man competition, yea, even as the Nattering Nimrods of North Avenue?

And the Great Dawgly Warriors maketh quick work of them, even unto ESPN, even unto the corny corps of the coarse and corseted Corso. And they shall be rained upon by the Gall Stones of Golston and the Pillaging of Pollack.

They shall be Mussed by Musa, and the Greene Machine shall mow them down, while the Shock Jocks shall Rock their Flock.

And lo, Ooga feeleth better, lo, even unto midseason verbal form, and blessed shall be his SAT score for his exploits of heroic vocabulary.

And long shall the People of the Dawg sheweth forth their exploits on the holy highlight reel.

Amen.

An Interview with Brian VanGorder

I've got to say I have traumatic Vietnam flashbacks whenever I reread this one. And I've never been near Vietnam.

2003

ATHENS—The name of Brian VanGorder was an obscure one a matter of months ago. Now he is a college football celebrity, and fans are eager to learn more about the energetic defensive strategist.

As we meet for our interview, the mustachioed mastermind of the Georgia defense allows himself a tentative smile, though the action is clearly painful to his jaw muscles. Relaxation and contentment, these things are unknown in his world.

After helping to bring the University of Georgia (13-1) its first conference championship in 20 years, the second-year DC says he's only just begun. To live. White lace and promises. "This year was all about learning to win," says VanGorder. "But that's only Phase One. Lots of programs know how to win."

So what's next for the Georgia Bulldogs? The coach sips from a mug and replies, "We've got to be more ruthless in the administration of the beatdown."

VanGorder points out that he holds a BA (Beatdown Administration) from Wayne State, where he lettered four years for the Festering Blood-Sucking Leeches of the Dry Rot Division of the Mid-American Wasteland Conference.

Beatdowns for Georgia have been few and far between in recent years. A scattered smattering of routs came only in the second half of the 2002 season. The third-ranked Bulldogs won too-close-for-comfort contests with Clemson, South Carolina, Alabama, and Auburn. But isn't a win a win?

"No!" hisses VanGorder through slightly gritted teeth, biting off a few hairs of his moustache and chewing on them abstractedly. "We're trying to prepare these kids for *life*. Life is a gigantic, reeking cesspool stocked with piranhas that can munch through a cow and eat its baby calf for dessert in five seconds. I've seen that on the Discovery Channel, by the way. Taped it and watched it several times. Changed my life, to be honest. Would you like to see it?"

"Perhaps later. We were on the subject of winning . . ."

"Right. Well, to paraphrase Coach Lombardi, winning isn't everything—it's the pitiless, soul-crushing beatdown that brings true inner peace. And that's what we want our young student athletes to learn, long after they leave football, as they go into their communities and lead fruitful social lives."

"Um, beatdowns—in their social communities?"

"Yeah—no, *hell* yeah," snaps the coach. "Beatdowns are a microcosm of life, baby. Take the piranha, faced with a plump, succulent moo-cow named Flossie . . ."

"Coach, how will the 2003 Dawgs be guided toward more fruitful, life-enriching beatdowns?"

"That's a good question," says the affable bloodshed enthusiast. "We have several platforms for better administration of the beatdown next season.

"It all begins with Coach Van Halanger in the weight room. We want mind-rupturing, obscenely-muscled freaks of nature. We want our kids to be on the fringes between psychopathic and bestial, bellowing for raw meat—slamming their heads against the wall during their week in The Hole, a facility we secretly maintain beneath the Butts-Mehre sub-basement."

"The Hole?"

"Of course, Dimwit! We want them gnawing on their own toes in there, fashioning crude weapons out of loose pavement stones. So they're like the thing in Alien, but less beautiful, dig?"

"Tell me about The Hole. You said . . ."

"I said nothing. You didn't hear it. Give me that tape. I know your children's names and where they go to school. Nothing personal.

"Anyway, back to the beatdown. We tell our linebackers, if you got no elemental fire-demons leaping from your butt when you break wind, don't bother to suit up. We want ravaging death angels. Even at the midfield coin toss, we want our kicker Billy Bennett to lunge onto someone's helmet, cling to the face-mask with his tiny placekicker fingers and toes, and bite their nose off.

"We'll get a few penalties, but these are learning experiences."

"Okay. What do your players learn in such experiences?"

"Who said anything about *our* players learning? I'm talking about the other guys. They will learn something, friend, an effective lesson they'll cherish for the few moments remaining in their feeble lives."

"Gotcha. So Coach, what's next in your beatdown regimen?"

"Next, we need to find the new team leaders. Jon Sullivan is leaving the nest. Flying off to wreak havoc on other nests, eat the eggs in them. That's how I prefer to think of it. Screech the death cry of the Whooping Sullivan Bird. Pardon me, I'm emotional. Okay, I'm fine. As I was saying, we need to anoint a new High Priest of the Beatdown."

"High Priest?"

"Basic football terminology. Do your homework," grumbles VanGorder impatiently. "Playbook 101 stuff. The High Priest of the Beatdown gives the incantation to invoke the Demon of Pain and Disfigurement. He presents the first blood offering. You can't play winning defensive football without a High Priest of the Beatdown. Then, of course, it all comes down to execution."

"Of course. Executing fundamentals."

"No, NO!" hisses VanGorder, shattering the ceramic mug inside his fist. "Executing opposing *players*. We want to lay down the SinisternMark of the Nasty Dawg on their loathsome yellow hides, something no soap will wash out and no opium can soothe. We want to implant the Rabid, Howling Mad Dawg Mojo right down in their bone marrow, so that sixty years from now, they're still waking up in their maximum care facility beds with their brains in a jar and identified only as 'John Doe Number 67, Offensive Tackle,' screeching their vegetable lungs out without knowing why. Nothing but pure animal terror remaining in their vacant souls."

I'm observing that it's clear this man is a poet of recreational terror. Briefly, the office door opens and Mark Richt calls in, "Bible study in five minutes, fellas! Don't be late."

Coach VanGorder swallows the last pottery shards of his coffee mug, then pauses to catch and eat a housefly using only his tongue. "Next year is definitely the Year of the Beatdown," he concludes.

"So I'd say your goals are high ones," I say. "Or low. Depending on the ethical orientation of the observer, I suppose. Anything else you're shooting for?"

"If we apply the Beatdown, release the turmoil of the Pain and Disfigurement Demon, lay down the Sinister Mark of the Nasty Dawg—these are good basic starting points for any program, from Pop Warner/Pee Wee to pickup games at your federal corrections facility.

"Beyond that, of course, we'd be interested in summoning the Four Horsemen of the Apukealypse, which are Fracture, Herniation, Laceration, and Disembowelment. When we get that done, I'll know we're administering the beatdown to the best of our God-given abilities. Now come along. You've expressed interest in The Hole. Strip down to your briefs, please."

"Really, it sounds fascinating, but I really have to be . . ."

"I said, come along. Say hello to my little friends, Odell and Thomas."

I Know Where You Sat Last Season

Green has been my color lately. You feelin' me? I'm talking about Moolah here. Crisp lettuce. Heavy wampum.

I'm happy to report I've come into a tidy little sum. You could say a whole delegation of dead presidents have convened in my bank account.

No brag, just fact. I've brought home more bacon than Porky Pig during rutting season. I've put away so many Simolians, I could be the lead prosecutor of Simolia.

"But Mr. Saxondawg," you ask. "We've always known you to be an intelligent, handsome, and globally idolized specimen of masculinity. But we didn't know you were a wizard of wealth as well. Tell us more! Relate how you've accumulated this tidy sum of money."

If you must know, I've collected my tidy sum through the ingenious exploitation of one simple wager, a bet I've made in leading taverns again and again. Never has it failed me, until the time it did. It was a good thing, but a parachute only has to fail once. Alas, I've decided to retire this one. That's why now, for the first time, I'm going to lay bare my secret for you, my loyal readers. I'll tell you my bet. Hold my beer.

Our story begins during my visit to your local watering hole. You know—the one where you and the guys get together for adult beverages. Imagine me there with you, hoisting a few and sharing pleasantries with fellow patrons. Laughter. Good times.

Quietly, I work the room, tuning in to various conversations until I identify the true Georgia fan in the room. There's one, of course, in every crowd, from the hills of Hiawassee to the quagmires of Quitman.

"I couldn't help but overhear you're a Dawg," I say, wrapping an arm around the guy. "An avid aficionado of the red and black. Which makes you the five-star standout on the roster of this here saloon! I salute you, my friend."

Fist bumps ensue. If the mood is right, barks, the sacred Munson quotes, and mutual backslaps flow as freely as the adult beverages.

"Allow me to buy the next round," I say after the canine revelries run their course. Then, as we wait for our libations of choice to arrive, I smile slyly and say, "I know where you sat last season."

"No way," he replies with a puzzled grin. "You and I have just met."

"All the same," I said, "I know where you sat last season. And your buddy Ulysses here says I can prove it."

With that, I slap a crisp fifty-dollar bill, featuring the visage of Union General Hiram Ulysses Grant, on the bar.

"Sir, you have lodged an offense to my sacred honor," he intones with gravity. "I come from a hallowed Southern family of many generations, and I will solemnly attest that the pub-crawling, lily-livered blue-belly on yonder note is no friend of mine." He peers down at Ulysses. Ulysses peers back, looking wistful about the alcohol present.

"Normally I would pull out a velvet glove and slap you with it," he continues, "Perhaps it would be pistols at dawn. But I must admit—you've got me curious! I'm certain I've never seen you anywhere near my seats at a game. So stranger, I'll take your bet."

He offers his hand. We seal the deal, and a small crowd begins to gather around us.

"So let's have it. Where did I sit last season?" he asks.

"Oh, I could give you section and row, take your money, and buy everyone here a round," I say. "Easy-peasy. But where's the fun in that? Let's take it up a notch. I'll identify pretty much everyone who sits around you."

People around us gasp. "Impossible!" harrumphs an old codger. "Even for Saxondawg, a globally idolized specimen of masculinity!"

"Go on," says my new friend, eyeing me suspiciously.

"Done. Your section, sir, with ladies first.

"You sit near a certain nice, elderly woman who comes with her husband. Always smiling, wants to know everything about your family. Pays no attention to the game, but performs a valuable public service by playing with that kid on your row, the one with ADHD who drives everybody crazy, going to the bathroom every single third down."

"Why, that's Mrs. Jenkins," he says with some degree of awe. "Perfect description."

"Yep, Mrs. Jenkins, that's her. But there's also that younger woman a few seats away. Now this one, she's *all* about football. Goes wild when the defense screws up. Leaps up, cusses like a sailor, and when something good actually happens, she crushes about five of your ribs while hugging you. Smells like bourbon and puts the fear of God into the third-down bathroom kid."

"Firewater Babs! Everybody knows Firewater Babs!"

"That's the one. Only person more gung-ho than Babs is Mr. Everybody-Up."

"You mean . . ."

"Yep. Mr. Everybody-Up. Sits, what, about three rows in front of you? Near that guy who projectile-vomits Varsity food once per season. The onion rings always come first, and you have to move out quickly after that. Anyway, I'm talking about the younger dude, Mr. EU, the one obsessed with getting the section behind him to stand up. Turns around and reams out that poor little octogenarian—"

"Old Mrs. Thistlegreen."

"—Who has arthritis and just wants to finish her knitting."

"Yeah! That's right! Personally, I stand up, but when it's the fourth quarter against Druid Hills Driver's Training, and UGA is up 83-2—I mean, come on. The guy is relentless. We don't call him Mr. Everybody-Up, though. For us, he's Jackass-in-the-Box."

"Yeah, I know. Didn't want to say his nickname in mixed company. But I've saved the clincher for last. Most famous guy in your section: The Human Bullhorn of Despair."

My friend spits out about half his drink. Of course, I've deftly stepped to the side just in time, and stayed dry. I've done this enough times that I anticipate every move.

"The Human—that's—why, you're talkin' about—"

"Yes sir, the Human Bullhorn of Despair. Gifted by nature with an extraordinarily loud, booming voice, though sarcasm is his true super power. His high-pitched cry of cosmic angst carries across vast distances, which is the real reason Georgia's coaches began wearing headphones in the '80s, soon after the Bullhorn began attending games. 'Way to go, DOOOOOO-ley!' 'Run da damn BALL, Goff!' 'Whattayathinkya DOIN', Donnan?' And his more recent classic, just a simple, 'RIIIIIIIIIIIIIICHT!' He works up a good loogie, a big spitwad, with that last one, then lets fly. His masterpiece."

My friend knows he's beaten. He's reaching for his wallet, ready to dole out fifty. But I'm just getting warmed up. "The legends say the Bullhorn's most miserable season was 1980. He was there in Jacksonville when Lindsey Scott broke the long one, and to him, the main point was that Lindsey actually screwed up. He should have cut to the right rather than the left on that touchdown run, and it would have been easier.

"The Human Bullhorn of Despair. Every new season people think he may be too old to return for another round of self-punishment; that his blood pressure finally pushed beyond physical limits, and just maybe the man exploded, bits of him peeling off the walls, because of that kid we missed on Signing Day. But he always shows up, sure as autumn follows summer. The worldwide evangelist of football-induced rage. Some say he was there in the 1890s, in Herty Field, for those very first . . ."

"That's enough, you've proven your point," says my friend, shaking his head. "Here's five tens: one, two, three, four, five. And to show no hard feelings, I got the next round."

I always thank him with a smile but excuse myself politely. I have to hit the highway and get to the next town and the next pub before people in *this* one begin sharing that it's odd how much this guy's section in the stadium sounds like their own.

I had a nice run. But all good things must come to an end. It happened in Ty Ty, down there in Tift County. It was a lively evening at Tall Bob's Snuff 'N Snort. You've been there, right? One of those cinder block joints on Highway 82, just past Cousin Goober's Fresh Melons and Handmade Injun Keychains Outpost.

Cousin Goober? He's about one-sixth Choctaw and two thirds Lower Alabaman, and a fifth of bourbon when he can get it. Tell him Saxondawg sent ya and he'll set you up with a complimentary honeydew melon. It's a breakfast orgy, I mean it.

Anyway, I was in Tall Bob's, nearly through my spiel, and I was hitting my target, same as it ever was. My new buddy was nodding along, awestruck, as I nailed everybody in his section. Looked like he was seeing a ghost. How could I know all this?

Then when I got to the Human Bullhorn, my big closing number, my new friend's eyes grew wide with alarm. His jaw popped open and a little trail of Skoal began inching down his chin. His hand was frozen in the act of reaching for his wallet.

As I finished my description, time seemed suddenly to slow down for me. A huge fist appeared right in the center of my line of sight, coiled and tight and intent on its business. In slow motion, the fist expanded until I was looking at hairy knuckles in full IMAX 3D. Last thing I remember seeing is a teeny, tiny little flea just south of his Ty Ty High senior ring.

And then the lights went out.

Next thing I knew, I was staring right at the ceiling, and there was a ring of faces peering down at me. My neck was kind of affixed to the floor by some alcoholic blend of superglue. It felt like a bomb had detonated on my face, and my nose may have been incinerated once and for all. Somewhere, somebody was moaning. I realized it was me.

The face of my new buddy emerged from the circle of onlookers, up there near the ceiling somewhere. He dropped a fifty-dollar bill, which grew larger as it fluttered down to my chest.

The guy spoke: "I don't know who you are or where you come from, mister. Maybe you're CIA Black Ops, to know so much about me. Maybe you're a time traveler or practicing the dark hoodoo arts. I don't know about all that.

"But I do know you're a damn liar! I never said Lindsey should've cut right instead of left, you jackass—I said he should have lateraled the dang ball back to Herschel. Numbskull was wide open!"

You can have the bet if you want it. I'm done with it.

Ooga vs. South Carolina, 2002

In the beginning, when the earth was young and the Big Dawg createth all the hordes of the world, those who were reeking and those who were of manly aroma, the league was without form and void, and a flatulent mist encircleth the great green gridiron of this earth.

And nasty was the stench of that mist, and it was called The Great Gas Bag of Lou. And many were the torments of this vaporous entity, for it speaketh to men in endless motivational speeches, culled from the scrolls of the cheese-laden prophet Tony Robbins.

And the Great Gas Bag of Lou moveth like the stale flapping of the great armpit of the earth, from the northern wastes to the southern waste and to every corner where people be wasted.

And the Gas Bag taketh the shape of a shriveled and gnarly balloon, and great were its wrinkles, like unto the late Granny Clampett.

And it sayeth endless trite sayings, then moveth on again, and the People of the Hog, and the Yankeeish Tribes of South Bend, and many others of the world's hordes endured the gasses and sigheth in relief when it passeth from their sickly hindparts into the air, leaveth its enduring stench, and moveth on.

And lo, the Great Gas Bag of Lou casteth about the earth for a place to emit its foul odor yet again, and behold, it findeth that wretched waste, a place reviled even by the lowly standards of Lower Carolina, yea, the land of Columbia.

And the Great Gas Bag descendeth yet again, and speaketh the words of infomercials, and fireth up the People Who Liveth in Vans Down by the River, who findeth the stench to be fragrant, and mistaketh Skippy the Heir to be a warrior of great wisdom.

And the people were filled with visions of adequacy, and dreameth dreams of rising to the heights of mediocrity, and from the depths of their bowels they yearned to be average. For lo, they were Chicken People, and short were their highlight films, and many times were they grilled, fried, baked, roasted, and nuggetized by the more savage and hungering warriors of the world.

But of their offseason cluckings there was no end.

Hear, O Chicken People!

Prepare Ye for the Merciless Whooping of thy Feed-Plumpened Hindparts!

Submit thy breasts, thighs, wings, and womanly dumplings for thy ritual basting!

The People of the Dawg seizeth ye by thy chickenly nuggets and loppeth off thy Jenkins.

Ye faceth no longer the feeble and girlish Cavalier People who mauleth thee even in their gigglesome youth. The Great Spiked Club of Ooga shall WAIL in two days' time, and it shall puncture the Great Bag of Gas, until the rumble of its hoary explosion of flatulence shall resound throughout the dung-strewn pastures of Lower Carolina, and the earth shall swallow up the Great Dead and Upturned Cockroach that men call Williams-Brice, and the resulting winds, they shalt carry away all thy thousand trailer parks of Lower Carolina.

And the People of the Dawg shall hear the merciful silence of no more motivational sayings.

Amen.

Recrootin' Targets

★ ★ ★ ★ ★ **Vezoovius Jackson,** DE, Goober's Fork, GA (Junior Samples High School). Blazing speed (4.25 in the 40), size (6-2, 310), and willingness to apply the beatdown (70 hours community service, five written apologies) are already making the little town of Goober's Fork a mecca for major college coaches and loaded Auburn boosters. Vezoovius has a 3.0 GPA, and a matching 030 on his SAT, which may need a little work.

★ ★ ★ ★ ★ **Werner "Howitzer" Goebbels von Blitzenpanzer,** K, Porto Alegre, Brazil (Reichstag Day School). Hans routinely booms 65-yard field goals, 70-yard punts, and dummkopfs who get in his way. Recruiters are hiring native guides and rafting down the Amazon to check him out, though Hans' family, who have lived in Brazil since 1945, are notoriously averse to publicity.

★ ★ ★ ★ ★ ★ **NaFarius Kelly,** WR, Atlanta (Al Capone High School). A rare six-star player, Nafarius is a receiver on the field and a distributor off it. "This should be his breakout year," says his coach. "Particularly if they move him to minimum security."

★ ★ ★ ★ ★ **MAGNIFICON®,** ATH, Miami (F. Castro Military Academy). Formerly known as Bubba Leon O'Toole, this versatile athlete has rebranded himself and already has his own line of action figures. "**MAGNIFICON®** plays ball, no joke," says **MAGNIFICON®**. "**MAGNIFICON®** also fights an ongoing war against crime by night as well as against his inner demons. Trains in the forbidden black arts in his spare time." He is studying star alignments and putting his ear to seashells to determine which eager university wins his services on the football field and in local crime-fighting. His mother/CEO, THE AWESOMAMATRON®, will play a crucial role in his decision as well.

★ ★ ★ ★ **Lester "Dump Truck" Caledonia,** DT, Hamhock, GA (Second Amendment Country Day). He has the size (6-11, 419) and should continue to grow past this, his latest eighth grade season. At age 29, however, The Dump Truck is a savvy veteran of football and his favorite sport, Cage Match Sumo Wrestling. Lester is known for his famed "dumping a load" sack technique.

Ooga's BYE Week

1999

Ooga the Hunkering Hermit, Spiked Bludgeon Hobbyist, Dealer of Double-Dawg Devastation and Six-Time Grand Champion of the Northwest Georgia Rancid Breath Tournament, hates many things.

He despises the warriors who come against him, including the Nattering Nimrods of NATS (North Avenue Trade School). He holds a bitter loathing for the demon spawn of Jan Kemp and all the unmanly sports, such as synchronized swimming, hacky-sack, cow-tipping, and dwarf-tossing.

But perhaps above all things, Ooga hates BYE weeks. During off-seasons, of course, he finds a comfortable den of grizzly bears and goes into hibernation. But off-weeks during the football season are odious to him. Generally, he ends up pillaging and burning some obscure peasant village on the order of Lavonia or Watkinsville. No one makes it out alive unless they happen to be on our target list of recruits. He stands among the ensuing ashes and rubble, letting forth a mighty wind of belching. Then he orders a pizza and smites the delivery boy.

A hunkering hermit has to do what he can. But it's not the same as Saturday Between the Holy Hedges of Dawgly Sanford.

This past weekend, Ooga crept out by the highway with the sole intention of weeping, wailing, and making evil hand and abdominal gestures at passing motorists. But then a northbound caravan came along, and his curiosity got the best of him. The hermit waited for the final vehicle in the caravan, an SUV packed with chattering yuppies, ran behind it, took a leap, and clung to its underside for two hours.

He had no problem summoning the arm and leg-strength to hang on for the duration, but his mind was cruelly assaulted by the smooth, soft rock stylings of Journey and Michael Bolton, wafting through the floorboard. No wizard could have concocted a torture so cruel. Soft rock is one of the little known weaknesses of the Dawgly warrior. Hendrix or a little death metal is okay by him. But absolutely no Journey or boy bands.

The yuppie passengers heard terrible shrieks and thought the transmission needed some work. But it was the howling of a prophet in agony.

Finally the vehicle came to a stop, and Ooga slid from his place of concealment. He found himself surrounded by a range of hilly places—and hordes of yuppies, battalions of them, reeking of unmanly cologne. Ooga now recognized it all for a trap! It looked as if the Vandified Hamster People of Gnashville, the Devourers of Quiche and Nibblers of Cheese, had summoned their minions from across the world. Ooga knew he could handle two or three hundred such feeble challengers with little problem. But here they were beyond counting—which, in the case of Ooga, is anything past 17, the total of his fingers and toes.

He knew a wise warrior would avoid drawing attention to himself. How could he blend in with such pasty-faced panty-waists and nancy-boys? His own ground-length beard was encrusted with stray bits of chipmunk and pepperoni. His loincloth was not fashioned by Gucci.

As he pretended to be a tree, he saw that the yuppie hordes were prancing to and fro, exclaiming oddly on the merits of the leaf colors; bantering with pumpkin and apple merchants; and screeching in ecstasy whenever one of them spotted a rotting barn with Coca-Cola painted on the side. He had heard of such folk, many of them from a strange, unholy land known as Dun-Woodee.

Even at a Clemson home game, Ooga had not beheld such mindless pagan activity. Worshipers of dead leaves! His mind struggled to comprehend it.

Finally, he decided the only sane course of action was to slay some of them. So he smote 47 yuppies and hung them from the trees about which they had chattered so rapturously. The designer colors of the smitten made a pleasing display among the oranges and browns of the leaves, though the survivors seemed not to appreciate it. He trudged home, humming "The Rains of Castamere" to himself in the contentment of a true warrior.

It was a strange and provocative weekend for Ooga, as off-weeks always are. He has vowed to enter the strange hilly regions of North Georgia no more. There lurketh madness!

TECHWAD: A Visit to the Huddle

November 2003

Odell Thurman shuddered as he wiped the blood from his hands. "Never fails," he said. "Messiest game of the year. Last season I showered four times after the game, and I still couldn't get all the ooshy, smushy stuff out of my hair."

"Oh, stop your moaning," said David Pollack, skipping up to the defensive huddle. "The tight end *still* has his hands inside my jersey. He never even bought me dinner. And doesn't he need to go back to his own side between plays?

"Look, I'm used to being held, but it creeps me out how some of the Tech players kind of *enjoy* it too much. It's disgusting. Say, what's with this game day crowd? I keep waving my arms to get them louder. I'd say they're only about fifty percent as loud as last week."

"Don't forget, we're in Tech's place," said Odell, spitting a piece of an ear into his hand. "That means there are a few *hundred* Tech fans scattered around, as opposed to maybe fifteen or sixteen of them at our place—HEY THORNTON, YOU BEEN MIKE-TYSONED," he suddenly barked, dropping the ear-chunk down the back of Bruce Thornton's jersey.

"Man, I *hate* it when you do that," said Thornton, trying to wiggle the detached organ out of the place where it had lodged in his pads, without actually touching the fleshy mass. "What am I gonna tell my lady if she finds it on me later? These things interfere with my cologne essence after a while."

"Skipping helps," said Pollack. "Man, I miss Boss Bailey. He always brought his toothbrush into the D huddle. Very good etiquette, that guy—these new dudes could learn something from him."

"Good tooth care is essential," said the Tech tight end, still hanging from Pollack's shoulders. "Otherwise you can get pyorrhea, gum disease, and—"

"Shut *up*!" said Pollack, shaking the player in his fist. "I told you to *ask permission* before talking. And call each of us 'Dawgly Overlord.' Like 'Dawgly Overlord Pollack'; 'Dawgly Overlord Davis'; and 'Dawgly Overlord Thurman.' Screw up again and I'll revoke your pass to attend our huddles."

"Yes, Dawgly Overlord Pollack," said the tight end obediently. "Please don't send me away. I like it here with—"

"Shut up," said Pollack. "Now. Who still doesn't have a sack?"

Several Scout Teamers and one cute blonde cheerleader raised their hands. "Oo! Oo! Me! Me!" said Thomas Davis, jumping up and down, bashing his way to the front.

"Davis, you've got six sacks, two picks, a safety, and a Federal Witness Protection applicant," said Pollack. "Be fair and let someone else have a chance. You're too selfish, that's your problem." Davis hung his head in shame and sniffed; Davis was known for his tender feelings.

Pollack continued, "Mrs. Richt, how 'bout you?"

"Nope, I got Reggie Ball on the last play," said the coach's wife. "I can't believe how easy it was to run him down. *And* I was carrying a tray of PowerAde at the time. That young man uses bad language, though. I had to give him an extra knee in his wind chimes."

"Say, where is Ball, anyway?" asked Pollack, peering at the Tech offensive huddle. The Jackets formed a small cluster of whining, moaning football players, some of them helping the others to stand up. One was taping his eyeglasses for the third time. Reggie Ball was not among them. Ace backup Nefarious Bilbo was missing, too.

"I last saw Reggie about six plays ago," said Davis. "I figured they took him out because the ball wasn't making it to the quarterback, so what was the point, right? I personally took the snap directly from the center twice. Those guys aren't too swift of foot."

Thornton broke into the conversation. "Hey, Odell, c'mon, man, wipe your feet before you come in here. You're *nasty*, dog. You stepped in a pile of something."

Thurman examined his right cleats, then his left. Slowly a broad smile began to spread across his face. "TECH-wad," he said, savoring the sound of it. "REGGIE bar. Who wants a bite?

"Well, that solves the Reggie mystery, anyway," said Pollack.

"Dawgly Overlord Thurman, could I have what comes off your cleats?" asked the tight end, reverently, offering the inside of his helmet. "He deserves a Christian burial."

"Shut up," said Pollack.

"Three out of six, three out of six," screeched Flag Boy from the empty Tech band section.

Obsessive Fixation Diary

An Off-season lament.

July 2004

Monday, July 12

Dear Diary, it's happening again. *I'm getting the fever.* Starting to tremble all over. I feel the cold chills, even though it's ninety-five degrees in the shade. I'm not eating well, and my friends and family keep asking if I'm listening when they talk to me.

Obsessive thoughts. I have to buy a new TV. I've watched certain videos so much that images have burned into my screen. Or maybe my eyeballs—I can't be sure. There's Sean Jones' 90-yard scoop-n-score against the Vols, and Odell's full-field pick-six against Auburn. They seem more real to me than this business meeting I'm sitting through.

Fifty-three days, twenty-one hours.

Wednesday, July 14

I'm trembling most of the time now. Football season, COME TO DADDY.

This morning I insisted on tailgating coffee break out in the company parking lot; the guys thought I was loony. Me? I think their conversations about fishing are loony. And the dang Olympics. They said they'd be in Athens so it got my interest. Who knew there's another Athens? There's no Odell in the Olympics. Call me when they add an Odell event.

The picture of Richt's face shaved into my chest hair is starting to come in, and I've got to say it looks *good*. Even the little scar above it sort of looks like a tiny halo. I did have to let my boss fire me because I won't work with a shirt on. Don't they get it? Classic art should not be covered up. Now I'm on the job market.

Fifty-one more days, seventeen hours.

Sunday, July 18

Went to church to ask for prayer as I seek gainful employment. Now I have to find a new church. Our preacher said, "Can I get an amen?" and I leapt into the aisle on all fours and gave him a "WOOF WOOF WOOF WOOF!"

They might have overlooked it if I hadn't bitten the organist right in the pianissimo. While I was at it, I marked my favorite pew as *my territory*. Dawgy style, right? No danger of anyone else claiming that seat now. Probably including me, because I got excommunicated. I'm told Baptists have never excommunicated anybody, and I'm the first. Cool to be part of history, I guess.

But who cares? WE'RE INTO THE FORTIES! Forty-seven more days until the PIGSKIN APOCALYPSE!

Thursday, July 22

Rogaine for Men, Manly Chest Edition rocks! Richt's portrait is so real, his eyes follow you across the room. I'm quite the hit at the local swimming pool. I was in the deep end, and a kid swimming by underwater opened his eyes, got a load of my belly, and almost drowned.

Too bad they can't see the proud, tattooed visage of Wally Butts on my butt. But even I'm smarter than to let the dawg out in that regard.

Time to start loading up the tailgate, because it's only FORTY-THREE DAYS until the good times roll! Man, times like this, the only thing that will calm me down is watching my little first-grader pummel a grown Tech fan. That's Daddy's Little Girl!

Wish I hadn't driven all those nerds out of the neighborhood. Young Odellina wailing on a Jacket fan is the only sport that even comes close to college football.

Saturday, July 24

Parked the car this morning, short walk from Sanford! WOO HOO! BRING ON GEORGIA SOUTHERN!

Amazing the parking spots you can grab if you come a month or so early.

There are no more than a thousand or so of us unpacking our grills and whatnot. (To be honest, some of these people are SQUIRRELY. I mean, I'm a fanatic when it comes to Georgia football, and I'm proud to admit it. But the guy who got the Jim Donnan lookalike facial surgery a few years back, that's got to be a drag for him now that Donnan's a panelist on a cable talk show.

That's why I went with the face of former coach Harry Mehre (UGA 1928-37). Nobody knows his face anyway. But *I* know, and that's what counts.

Larry tapes are cranked and ribs are on the grill. I'm being extra, extra nice to my wife this week. Even listening when she talks at me occasionally, nice things like that. I know she's expecting our next child sometime in mid-August, so she deserves a little pampering.

We're crossing our fingers and hoping little Pollack Odell VanGorder Saxon doesn't make his entrance to this world until the first BYE week, which is September 27, the week after LSU. It would be a whole month late, but I can't face another baby before that. My wife is a great gal, really, but she's a bit of a wimp when it comes to spending her third trimester living in the backseat.

I tell her that when the magic moment comes, she'll do great. Nature and Georgia football loyalty will take over. We've gone through this with each of our nine children, from our oldest, Hines Bobo Saxon, to tiny li'l Greene Brown Blue Saxon.

Speaking of which, several of the above are choking each other right now, so I need to sign off.

This is goodbye, diary. The trembling and cold chills are coming on, and I won't be capable of writing or speaking articulately or going to the bathroom after today.

Ooga vs. Northwestern State, 2002

Hear these words, Demons of Northwestern State! Your feeble obscurity irritateth the prophet! For is not Louisiana in the Southeasterly wastes? Doth this not mean thou art truly Northwestern Southeastern? Doth not thy school have a Geography Department?

Your puny attempts to confuse the Big Dawg are wretched and worthy of a Pollackly Pummeling, and it shall be administered, in northern quarters, southern quarters, eastern quarters, western quarters, and hindquarters. The horns of thy demons shall be extracted, and thy pitchfork shall be inserted deep within those valleys where the sun shineth not.

And the People of the Dawg shall unleash all manner of whoopitude upon thy hideous and womanly hindquarters, until thy runneth away unto the furthest corners of Northwestern Southeastern, only to findeth out you have used all four corners already. Ye can runneth but ye canst not hide! The Big Dawg openeth a big can of Pollack on thy I-AA feebleness, until thou shalt pray for Tulane to reveal unto you its own place of hiding.

And the People of the Dawg shall tailgate forth, and imbibest grog both domestic and imported, and taketh unto themselves comely wenches, and be in general the coolest and most studly of all the reeking tribes.

And lo, the great ranking of the People of the Dawg shall increase. For thou canst not spell Pollack without "poll." Amen.

Greg Blue Knocks USC QB Into Next Week

September, 2004

During Lou Holtz's final scintillating season in Rooster World, there was a thrilling chicken-choke against the Dawgs. The Gamecocks jumped to a big lead, then watched UGA storm back to take the game in the fourth quarter. At a critical point in those final moments, Greg Blue met SC's Pinkins (not to be confused with Jenkins, the previous forgettable guy) and laid down a hit for the ages. He brought enough wood that Noah could have built an ark from it in the middle of the stadium. Here's an alleged newspaper account of the pop—long before targeting—heard round the world.

(From Wire Reports)

COLUMBIA—The impact reverberated through the University of South Carolina's Williams-Brice Stadium. Millions of viewers of the CBS Southeastern Conference Game of the Week, as well as 85,000 fans in attendance, could hear the pads pop.

On a game-turning play at the Georgia 7-yard-line, Bulldog safety Greg Blue met USC quarterback Dondrial Pinkins at the line of scrimmage and commandingly denied him a crucial first down, forcing a fumble in the bargain. From there, Georgia's stout defense was able to hang on to its 4-point lead after storming back from a 16-point first half deficit with 20 unanswered points.

But not until today did it become clear just how powerful Blue's hit was. The blow actually knocked the Gamecock signal-caller into next week.

Tuesday afternoon, Pinkins, a native of Camilla, Ga., suddenly turned up in the men's room of the University of South Carolina Student Union. The fifth-year senior was reportedly recoiling in pain, and still dressed in a game-soiled uniform and pads. And he was ripe, even for a bathroom stall.

Sophomore Dusty Tewksbury of Irmo, SC reported, "It was, like, spooky, you know? I was like, just sitting there in the stall reading the graffiti and taking care of business, when suddenly there was Dondrial, right there in the stall. He seemed kind of out of it, and he yelled, 'Yow,' which echoed really big. Then he said a cuss word, right out loud. One that wasn't written on the wall."

Pinkins could offer no explanation. "All I know, I turn upfield and see this big huge number 17 in my face, then, I'm in the can with a dude and it's Tuesday, you know?" (Just before that last park, Pinkins mumbled something. When asked several times to repeat what he'd mumbled, Pinkins finally said, "Okay, Okay, I had a blackout, okay? Ha ha. Very amusing."

Saturday was "Black Out Day" for fans at Williams-Brice stadium.

Pinkins continued, "Least I missed my Monday test in Fun With Popsicle Stick Crafts."

Gamecocks Coach Lou Holtz reported that he was not aware of his starting quarterback's time travel escapade, but that "Georgia knows what they need to do to win. I'm trying to change the culture and the laws of physics here, show them we can manipulate time and relativity, too. Our guys just have to believe." When asked who the quarterback was that finished the game in Pinkins' uniform, Holtz said, "You got me. One of our quarterbacks is no more inept than the next. Pinkins, Jenkins, Stinkins?"

In other news, it was reported that Bulldog safety Thomas Davis hit running back Cory Boyd so hard that Boyd's third cousins once removed felt it.

The cousins live in Elklip, Minnesota. Medical authorities are investigating.

The Jacket-Hater's Alphabet

A is for Athens, a Southern-fried heaven,

B is for Bobo, 1997.

C is Chan Gailey (is he still alive?),

D is for Dooley, who won his first five.

E is Erk Russell, reborn as K. Smart.

F is for Flag Boy, a wimp off the chart.

G is for Gurley, set loose in OT,

H is for Herschel, who stomped them times three.

I is for insects, with very few wins.

J is for Johnson, all five of his chins.

K is for Kanon, from 34 yards,

L is for Lewis: we love our Grizzards,

M is for Munson, the Dawgliest tone,

N is North Avenue, ugly crime zone.

O is O'Leary, whose lies brought his fall,

P is for Pollack, still chasing R. Ball,

Q is for quit, as they did in '02.

R is for Richt, who still owns GTU.

S is their State, as in what we still run.

T is for Tickle pile, Tech's only fun.

U is for Uga, the mascot who reigns,

V is Verron, and 200 for Haynes,

W, Wansley, who caught Godsey's throw,

X is eXpel, the Tech Ten had to go,

Y, You Can Do That, and lose once again,

Z is for Zeier. He killed 'em. Amen.

Ooga vs. Alabama, 2002

October, 2002

It was still early in the season of 2002 when the Dawgs headed to Tuscaloosa for a showdown. Georgia was undefeated, but Pat Dye, who had coached Auburn and played for Georgia, was skeptical. On the Finebaum radio show, mercifully available only on radio in those days, Dye said that he didn't think the Dawgs were "man enough" to hang with the Tide. The rest, of course, is glorious red and black history. Ooga joined the team in taking up the challenge.

And lo, the People of the Dawg turned their eyes to the western wastes, where dwell they who call themselves the People of the Tide, though there are no tides near their dwelling, for there are no oceans, and lo, they are sorely confused about their habitat, like unto their mortal enemies the Tiger Eagles of the Jungle Plain.

And being thus confused, and having no prophet of their own, the People of the Tide sendeth forth their tosspot, he who is surly when he indulgeth in too much grog, and who speaketh abominations, saying that lo, the People of the Dawg *be not manly enough.* Then he belcheth forth and passeth into a stupor, which rendereth him more likeable for a few hours, though equally smelly.

And the People of the Dawg heareth his mocking words, and giveth forth a growl, and the holy hedges trembleth, and sacred Sanford quaketh, and somewhere Erk Russell spitteth forth lightning and emitteth thunder from his bowels. And Ooga, he who hunkereth, heareth also, and cryeth out:

Behold, People of the Tide, ye who were once a fearsome race, marching forth as the People of the Bear, a truly reeking but respectable horde. The Bear liveth no longer, except in limited edition lithographs, and 10,000 trailer park urchins who beareth his name, and several hundred who beareth his genes, and countless morons who beareth his face in the tattoo thereof.

Now thou art merely the People of the Tide, a leading laundry detergent, and ye speaketh forth of the Tide Rolling, though neither oceans nor washing machines roll, neither do elephants, which belongeth in the Jungle, which is where the Tiger Eagles dwell, for thou art a confused and vexing people, though Ooga liketh two or three of the comely cheerleader wenches, preferably simultaneously.

Thou art not only a confused people but also a DOOMED one, for the People of the Dawg art a MANLY ENOUGH People, and are summoned forth to prove out their manliness on network television.

And the People of the Dawg shall bring forth their manliness upon the field of battle, and your stadium shall fill with blood and the curdling shrieks of melon-bellied bubbas and big-haired trailer wenches until Ooga, the prophet, surfeth home on a Crimson Tide of thy seeping entrails.

And Richt the Righteous, who is also manly enough, shall take a short break from being righteous to pulleth the heart from the chest of his vanquished foe, and eateth it before the television cameras, just before the Pizza Hut commercial.

And then the People of the Dawg shall proceed to the Jungle Plain, where dwelleth he who strappeth on no pads but talketh big about manliness.

And the Big Dawg shall lift his leg and marketh him in liquid gold for territorial rights in November.

And the Elephant People of the Crimson Ocean Detergent shall return to their trailer parks, and changeth forth the diapers of young Bear VII and little Bearina, and prayeth before their limited edition lithographs that their Guardian Bear might come down once more and protecteth them from the fury of a Dawg who is surely MANLY ENOUGH.

Amen.

Scrimmagin' with the Ol' Ball Coach

2005

Steve Spurrier, the Evil Genius, is returning from exile.

After a historic run of excellence with the Florida Gators, he stormed the nation's capital and led the Washington Redskins to an incredible 7-9 record and then, in Year 2, to the inspiring heights of 5-11—though Spurrier has assured us that it was all someone else's fault.

For the beloved pigskin pilot known to some as Darth Visor, 2004 was a season of brooding in the darkness of Castle

Spurrier, peering at his crystal ball as his army of flying monkeys chattered around him.

"I'll get you, Jeremy Foley," he still mumbles occasionally. "And your little dog, too."

Speaking of dogs, Spurrier comes to Athens this year for another shot at his favorite nemesis. As we meet for our interview, we find the Ol' Ball Coach feisty and restless. (Spurrier corrects me and says it's *Head* Ball Coach, since he is not and will never be Ol'. Though he is sixty years ol'.)

The '66 Heisman Trophy winner stands in front of his desk, swishing air tee-offs onto the links of his imagination.

He hasn't lacked for interview requests lately. The world is curious about his SEC comeback. Rather than indulge in yet another interview, as less imaginative writers might do, we opted for something a bit different. We proposed the idea of a computer-based challenge: EA Sports' new edition of NCAA Football for Xbox. A born competitor, Spurrier was quick to accept, though he may or may not be clear on what a computer game showdown entails.

Ol' Ball Coach: So this is one of them rattlin' toy fields with the plastic men that go 'round in circles, right? You won't stand a chance, you know that.

Saxondawg: No sir, see? I'm hooking this console up to your TV screen. It's *digital* football rather than electric. I'll play the part of Central Florida, since that's your opener and your debut in Columbia. You'll be the Gamecocks, of course.

OBC: Gamecocks . . . Say what? Ha, ha, ha. You media guys. Pullin' the Head Ball Coach's leg. Seriously . . .

Sax: I'm completely serious. South Carolina's your new team, after all, um, right?

OBC: South Carolina? That the one near the Augusta Course? You know . . . I think you're right. Just wrappin' my head around the job. Hey, media guy, any idea if I actually *signed any contractual agreements* for this gig? I mean, like, legally binding and all?

Sax: Pretty sure you did, Coach. Let's get started. Hold your controller like so. We'll give this right here a click and—see? You've kicked off to me. My UCF Golden Knights are setting up a return.

OBC: Gimme that thing. Head Ball Coach gonna throw it around the yard. Watch me go. Fun'n' gun-it, pitch'n' catch. Have I ever told you the one from back in '66, my Heisman year, when—

SD: Wow! I returned the kick for a touchdown! Central Florida 7, Gamecocks 0.

OBC: Wait a minute. The Head Ball Coach wasn't ready. What kind of mascot is that on your side? Looks like a fat ball of Crisco. Needs his fanny kicked.

Sax: That's not the mascot, Coach. That's UCF head coach George O'Leary. I like the rendering myself. Don't you think the wiggling cellulite and the red-faced scowl are realistic? And look, they've even rendered a tiny résumé sticking out of his back pocket, with the lies scratched out on it. While we're at it, what do you think of your new stadium? Williams-Brice. See, we can pan the camera—

OBC: They left out the big ol' orange panel with "Welcome to the Swamp" written on it. How'd they forget that?

Sax: Focus, Coach, focus. South Carolina Gamecocks. Look down at the emblem on your shirt whenever you forget.

OBC: HA! . . . Ha, ha. Smartass fish-wrap scribe. Gonna lay it on ya now, take off the kid-gloves. Like I did in the big Tulane game in my Heisman year. Have I told ya that one? Watch my razzle dazzle on your kickoff.

Sax: Dang! What a hit! Your return man drops it, my guy scoops it! Dances into the end zone—it's a muff-six. Oops! Here's your visor back, Coach. I think you accidentally tossed it.

OBC: Let's see if there are any other channels on this TV, what say? Hey, kid, I ever tell ya what FSU stands for? Free Shoe—

Sax: Yeah, I think we've all heard that one by now. Also the line about Auburn's library and the coloring books. You can tell the Ray Goff one again if you really want to, I guess. If you don't mind my saying so, don't you think it's time to move on from the Florida stuff?

OBC: Truth is, I told ol' Prune Face, Jeremy Foley. the package I needed for comin' back to Florida. Take it or leave it, if you want the ol' coach to come toss it around the yard at UF, pitch'n' catch, fun it, gun it. The Gator fans, they remember my Heisman. Good people. To them, I'm a legend. Beloved. Hey, I got that ol' Heisman right over here, I'll let you take a picture with it—

Sax: All due respect, sir, I heard Foley replied to your offer, "You can't spell UF without FU." Let's get back to the game. We're at 14-0 on Xbox. Now that you see how it works, we should see some Evil Genius strategy, right?

OBC: Yes sir. Evil Genius strategy is, stick in Wueffel, maybe Shane Matthews, pitch'n'catch. Which button does that?

Sax: None. You got to use the guys that X-Box gave you. See, here's Blake Mitchell, for example.

OBC: (Pinches mouth inward, makes extended sigh, looks at ceiling.) See, this is what happened in DC. Right here. Same blasted thing. Owner won't let the ol' coach play his own game. Interferin' with personnel matters. Now, you sayin' some computer geek is tellin' me who I can play? Needs his fanny kicked.

Sax: Here's your visor again. You gonna call the play?

OBC: HA! . . . Ha, ha—no, gonna call a few Bull Gator boosters, good folks, hit the fairway. (Air-swings again, using controller as a golf club.) Which one of these buttons calls my Bull Gators? Did you say we're near Augusta?

UGA's Absolutely Perfect Day: Hour by Hour

In which every kind of good thing finally happens to Georgia fans, all at once. Or at least, this is how it ought to work.

December, 2005

SUNDAY, DECEMBER 4, 2005

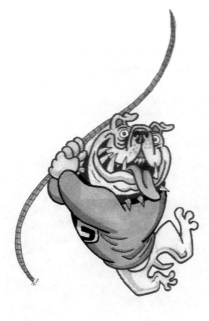

4:00 AM: Still inside the Georgia Dome, UGA fans continue to celebrate a second triumphant SEC championship in four years. Final score: Georgia 34, LSU 14. Ushers implore Dawg fans to stop barking, lifting their legs on stuff, and go home. Several ushers bitten in leg.

6:00 AM: Negotiations between Georgia Tech and Atlanta's Chick-fil-A™ Peach Bowl break down. Peach rejects Tech's offer of a free hot dog and coke to each Chick-fil-A™ Peach Bowl committee member ("Pig meat? Really?"), and a stuffed Chan Gailey doll that says, "CHANN-TASTIC!" when its "channy"-ring™ is pulled.

8:00 AM: Announcement that UGA President Michael Adams remains missing since conclusion of UGA-Kentucky game, when he is known to have walked across campus without his regular convoy of 17 armed bodyguards.

10:00 AM: UGA fans begins to head for the exits of the Georgia Dome, but continue celebrating a second triumphant SEC championship in four years. Each one insists on bestowing a "How 'bout them Dawgs" on every other fan in attendance, so this takes a long time.

12:00 PM Gaylord Music City Bowl in Nashville announces it will look for some team other than Georgia Tech for its prestigious matchup. Pretty much any team with six wins may apply.

1:00 PM UGA President Mike Adams is found wedgie-wrapped to a toilet pipe in Athens' Stegeman Coliseum; whimpers that university justice will prevail upon the five to ten thousand users of that toilet stall who came, took care of business, and ignored his plight.

3:00 PM UGA fans decide not to head for parking lots after all; break into concession areas, have big old Coke-and-tater-chip brunch to celebrate a second triumphant SEC championship in four years.

5:00 PM MPC Computers Bowl (Boise), Meineke Car Care Bowl (Charlotte), Red Man Chaw Bowl (Fort Smith, Arkansas),

EverQuest Online Fantasy Role-Playing Classic (E. Hobbiton) issue joint announcement that Georgia Tech will not be invited to any of their bowls or "classics," and that athletic director Dave Braine should please go home and leave them alone.

5:01 PM Dave Braine announces deal for the Georgia Tech Yellow Jackets to play in the Pennsylvania Amish Bowl, which is played in a cornfield in prayerful silence, with no television, no tackling, shaming, or beard-pulling, and which gifts players with plow parts. On the positive side, Tech is a 1-point favorite over the Amish pick-up team of elderly farmers and their wives.

6:00 PM UGA fans lift Georgia Dome from its foundations and parade it through downtown Atlanta, in celebration of Georgia's second triumphant SEC championship in four years. Still no one is ready to go home. Search for a very large-capacity Waffle House ensues.

8:00 PM Suspect in gas station robbery in Waycross, GA, is identified as Jan Kemp, a former UGA college tutor. Posse and hounds released to pursue Kemp through mosquito and reptile-infested swamp. Villagers arrive with pitchforks and torches. Vince Dooley commands the posse.

10:00 PM Judge rules that due to an odd technicality in Herschel Walker's original New Jersey General contract, he has one year of college eligibility remaining; also that in his view, Herschel "can still kick ass."

11:00 PM You personally receive word that a distant Swedish aunt you never knew you had has died and bequeathed her substantial Swedish meatball fortune and network of German beer breweries to you.

12:00 AM Those UGA fans who are still conscious get into brawl with waitresses at downtown Waffle House for refusing to set the clock to 13:26, which would reflect their 34-14 triumphant score in their second triumphant SEC championship in four years.

Jacket Game Day! You Can Do That!

The most requested Vent repost, every November. There is no date because I've updated it so many times to keep up with the latest Tech head coaches. I have no idea when it was actually written, but it was intended as the Tech version of a classic Vent post from IBDawg about game day in Athens, called, "Seven Notes on a Trumpet."

You wake up in the top bunk, beneath your Star Trek bedsheets, with that feeling in the pit of your stomach. That pounding feeling, that giddy, nauseous rush that can mean only one thing. You rush to the potty and take care of business. The feeling goes away.

But everything about tinkling—the color, the sound— makes you remember: Yellow Jacket football today!

You put on your best yellow sweater and yellow knee-socks, though you call them "gold," of course. Then, moving to the dresser, you specially polish your thick glasses, adding one final flourish—fresh tape wrapped around the bridge!

Speaking of bridges, your braces are also polished to a fine sheen. Braces for impact! New zits are popped, and you're lookin' *good*. You're lookin' *Jacket*.

Heart pounding, you race up the steps from your parents' basement. Mumsy and Pops are reading mail from the old home country, New Jersey, where they hope to return someday. You slip out the door quietly and pedal your three-speed through the crisp autumn air, game day flags a-flappin' from the handlebars. And there it is, just ahead—the MARTA station. It won't be long now!

You climb onto a southbound train, your eyes scan the car, and—yes! There, sitting next to the chatty transvestite—a man wearing yellow!

You make your way over and wave your pom-poms at him and giggle, and he says, "$#%^ off, you freakin' %$$^&!"

And now you feel it more strongly than ever—the essence of being a Tech fan. You giggle again more shrilly, dance away, then slide around safely under the seats, where he's not brave enough to grab at you and get who-know-what all over his hands— until the stop at North Avenue. You're tee-heeing for all you're worth as you elude the grasp of your tormentor and his switchblade. It's sort of like Frodo hiding from the Black Riders, right here on MARTA!

You disembark at the station, snatching quarters from a few homeless men, and take a deep breath of downtown Atlanta air—Tech air, the kind you can smell!

Now you see veritable *swarms* of other Jackets—*two* of them, *three* of them, nervously making their way through the station. Stranger danger!

Stranger danger! But that's all right. Most of them seem to be struggling just to walk without tripping; they won't hurt you.

Skipping along past the Varsity, you pause on the bridge over the Downtown Connector to indulge in a Tech tradition: spitting on cars passing underneath. It's a massive traffic jam of red vehicles heading north, and you nail an RV with a big loogie from your morning Yoo Hoo Soda. *Tee hee!* Saliva, the GT beverage of choice!

Then you're in heaven—on campus, a block from the stadium. Literally tens of thousands of computers in every direction. Calculus formulations and quantum physics being discussed with passion and accuracy. Slide rules whirring.

But most of all, you take in the grand pageantry that is game day. Game day! so many things . . .

It's the gray, smoggy sky; the deep blue of the police siren; the giggling of the frat boys enjoying an impromptu tickle pile on the sidewalk.

It's the sound of warring pimps and their now familiar Uzi-fire.

It's the hot campus chicks with their thick makeup, standing on the street corners and bartering with the passing cars. Odd that none of them seem to attend lectures.

It's the voice of Wes Durham, going into convulsions over a one-yard gain.

It's the giant rubber bee, ol' George O'Leary's former bathtub toy, patched all over, making funny farting sounds as the air oozes out yet again. You'll keep patching it up, like you do everything else. You're Georgia Tech! You can do that!

It's Chan Gailey, chantastic headphones weighing down his tiny, troubled head as he realizes he'll never once beat the Georgia Bulldogs, though his place in history is secure as "that 51-7 guy."

It's Paul "Fish Fry" Johnson, scowlin' and cussin' because he's far too brilliant for such a world as ours. In a better world, he would win big, but it's the world's fault, not his, that he doesn't. It is what it is, Paul. It is what it is.

It's Flag Boy, the aspiration of all Tech males. Tee hee!

Above all, it's six notes on a trumpet. You hear them now, playing the hallowed music, the sacred music, the Hymn of the Bee. There it is now, and you lift your voice to join in, pimples tingling, warm tears fogging your thick glasses. The whole stadium sings solemnly, and every one bobs up and down with each note, as you hear the wonderful rattling of their braces and glasses:

"When you say Buuuuudweiser . . ."

Those six notes on a trumpet, played by rented 45-year-old musicians; your call to Jackethood, setting your yellow, bee-wing heart and tiny little dangling stinger aflutter.

Deep down you know this is the year—the year you extend your streak against FCS teams. You friggin' *own* FCS teams!

The year you road-trip to a *brand spankin' new startup bowl* for the holidays—maybe even farther west than ever before, in Alaska—or maybe Okinawa! The year your first, long-awaited pubic hairs break the surface.

This sacred moment cannot last. Someday, By The Great Pointed Ears of Leonard Nimoy, you will be in the fatherland—in New Jersey. In Michigan. In Hong Kong.

Someday, swashbuckling your way through the business world with your slide rule raised in triumph, you will buy your parents a house with a bigger basement for you to live in.

But some things won't change. In your heart, you'll always be a Tech Guy—a proud drop in the endless river of yellow!

Ooga vs. Tennessee, 2002

Behold the carcasses of the Elephant Men. Do they not rot in yonder Tusk-came-loosa, on the field of Dawgly Conquest, at the hindward, liquidly leg-marked path of they who are manly, they who bring merciless chaos in the stadiums of their foes, they who are the Rampaging Road Warriors, yea, the PEOPLE OF THE DAWG?

And the grimacing grog-guzzling pie-hole of Dithering Dye the Debunked, hath not that oozing orifice been shut forth?

And the nattering naysayers of the reeking hordes of the Pigskin Punditory Nation, have they not been reduced to gigglesome geeklords? How thou likest us now?

The People of the Dawgs, the Manly Maulmeisters, came, they saw, they exacted forth the whippity-whopfest of the wailing whooparama.

But lo, what heareth the ears of the prophet from the rocky places where dwell the Hickolian Hill People, the minions of the wallowsome whalish warlords Lulu and Junior?

The prophet heareth the wheezy, whinesome whimpers of they who plead for mercy, unworthy of the Dawgs of War! Sir Casey of Malibu, he of the hair as spiked as Ooga's club, yet fashioned of mousse rather than steel—does he not moan about his sissified shoulder?

And King Kelley the Konceited, does he not groan about his nebulous knee? And the girlish minions of the battle-scarred bench, do they not cower in their womanly whirlpools just in time to AVOID THE WRATH OF THE RAMPAGING DAWGS?

Come forth, Prissy and Panicking Poltroons! Art thou Vols MANLY? Come forth if thou hast the Volleyballs of manhood! Cower not beneath thy blubbersome coach's pumpkinish parka!

Behold, it matters not who dresseth out among thy Crop of Craven Creamsicles. Bring forth Peyton the Heismanless, or Jamal the Jerkly.

Bring forth thy decade of dundering defenders. Buyeth some new warriors and taketh forth thy best shot. The People of the Dawg have smote thee TWICE, with fewer warriors from the zone of blue-chipperliness.

The People of the Dawg have smote thee with the Rage of the Rising Richtian Rampagers.

The People of the Dawg have smote thee with the Hellish Havoc of the Hobnailed Boot.

And the People of the Dawg just warmeth up.

Come taste the Pounding of Pollack the Pulverizer.

Come see thy orificial orange ooze beneath the blistering blades of the Greene Machine.

Come feel the cleats of Musa the Merciless, of Sullivan the Sackmeister, of Itty Bitty Billy Bennett the Bootmaster, of Damien the Demon and Terence the Terrible.

Surely the reeking orange entrails of the vanquished shall seep from the sanctuary of Sacred Sanford, and clog the outgoing highways upon which thy mooing minions shall flee in chaos.

And Fulmer the Foul shall blame forth the referees, and blame forth the players, and blame forth the circus tent canvas manufacturers which provideth his pumpkinish parka.

And the People of the Dawg will stand forth upon the high and rocky places, howling at the moon, crying forth, "Is there no more worthy challenger, no reeking horde manly enough to stand proudly before the Dawgly Decimators?"

And the People of the Dawg shall rule the regions of the Southeastern Kingdoms forever and ever. Amen.

Chicken Shop Closeout Sale

June 2006

Have you done your Father's Day shopping?

Try these last minute gift ideas from the Gamecock schlock stock!

GAMECOCK HOME VIDEO

IF ONLY: The Gamecocks' Greatest Moral Victories. (29.95)

- Crow it loud and proud: "We play you close every year!" Here are highlights of favorite games the Cocks almost won. See three-and-a-half quarters of winning football in each memorable moral victory.

WE ARE THE RETROACTIVE CHAMPIONS: Great Gamecock Achievements We Didn't Know About Until Recently. (29.95)

- The year 1996 saw the Gamecocks crowned as national champions—we just didn't realize it at the time. See terrific footage of all Steve Spurrier's great games, computer-colored to replace blue and orange with garnet.

CHICKENWEAR

Game Day T-Shirt: (19.95) Front side reads, "LOOK OUT! HERE COME THE GAMECOCKS!" The back reads,

> "You better thank your lucky stars for that
> _____ last-minute fumble!"
> _____ crooked call by the refs!"
> _____ freak once-in-a-lifetime play your guy made!"

Laundry marker provided. Simply take the shirt to the game, check the right slot at game's end, and scurry home to brood over what could have been! Available in sizes medium, large, and chunky chicken.

BOOKS

Wait 'Til Next Year: The Complete Story of Gamecock Football with All the Highlights, Immortal Moments, and Beloved Memories. (4-page booklet) (0.79) Order in BUUUULK bulk bulk bulk . . .

The Gamecock Application Bible with Steve Spurrier's taunts in red ink. (49.95) Special features applying the Bible to the teachings of Coach Spurrier, and tips for living every day with the wisdom of the master, providing he's not on the golf course and feels like helping. (Paintings accompanying the text: "The Taunting Samaritan"; "Noah Abandoning the Ark When It Wasn't Fun Anymore"; "Jesus Trash-Talking the Pharisees").

SPECIAL, MARKED DOWN: *The Gamecock Application Bible* with Lou Holtz's words in red ink (9.95) Special features applying the Bible to the teachings of Coach Holtz, and tips for living every day with the wisdom of the LOOUUUU. (Painting: "Lou Motivating the Disciples as Their Boat Sinks in the Storm.")

SPECIAL, ~~MARKED DOWN~~ / ~~WAY DOWN~~ / <u>FREE</u>: Plush cuddly Brad Scott doll. (~~0.29~~ COME GET 'EM). Just the gift for the little peckers in your family. Pull the chatty ring and he offers several cute postgame rationalizations.

Letter to Richt from the Omniscient Fanboy

Nothing spikes activity on the Dawgvent like a good quarterback controversy.

August, 2006

Dear Coach:
I just knew you would do it, sooner or later.

I knew you would make The Big Mistake. I wish you could see me sitting here rolling my eyes. (I've attached a digital photo to take care of that.)

It's *so* frustrating for a guy like me, knowing that I could help you so much in your job. Not that I was surprised when I failed to hear from you this weekend, before you announced your quarterback selection. I long since stopped waiting for you to hit me up on Facebook when something big is brewing.

My brain is being *wasted* by the Georgia football program.

Sometimes I feel so full-to-bursting, that I think deep, thick football wisdom is going to start trickling out of my ears or shooting out my nose, like the lunchroom milk does when my man Loogey Lufavich does his chimpanzee-eats-a-jalapeño imitation.

You see, Coach, you're not dealing with some typical NCAA fanboy. I'm a genuine, football-savvy, been-to-the-arena-got-the-tee-shirt fanboy.

No brag. Just fact. I played YMCA football, started one out of three years, and was second assistant to the trainer for the junior varsity this season at my school.

Yes, I've been to the wars. But it doesn't stop there. I am *undefeated all-time* on PlayStation. Let that sink in.

And yes, even on Super-Ditka-Expert Mode, which I played once because Beginner Mode is for babies—I can beat the game, like, infinity zillion to zip on Beginner Mode. And like my man Loogey says—it ain't braggin' if you can do it.

As for the Dawgs, I keep a close eye on the program by reading the newspaper every single day and getting scrimmage results off the Internet. And yes, I attended G-Day in person, where I saw all the players in action for more than thirty-five minutes until my dad said his butt was sore and we had to leave. Just from that, I got what I needed to lay down a big truth bomb.

Did you notice I mentioned the Internet? (The big word on the third line of the last paragraph.) I don't know if they have it in your football office yet, but it's a place on my computer where a whole mess of smart people post. There's, like, infinity quadrillion geniuses on the Internet, most of them on a place called The Vent.

You would not believe how famous I am on the Vent, and admired, too. One time one of my posts was right next to one by the mother of a player. So I'm what you might call an insider.

Anyway I made a Bank-On-It post several months ago. Let me explain. A Bank-On-It post is where you say what's going to happen, who's going to win, when the hammer's coming down on Auburn, that kind of thing. Then you say either "Bank on it" or "Mark it down." Both are binding before God, like a pinky promise. Personally I'm a Bank-On-It man.

Well, here's the deal. Back in April, I let all my Vent buddies know exactly what quarterback will start for our 2006 season. Then I sealed it with a Bank-On-It. I gave all my reasons, based on watching every play of G-Day except the parts we missed because of Dad's butt, which was the whole second half. (My dad is lame, what else is new?)

When I told all those wanna-be-me fanboy dummies (who drool while I rule) exactly who would play quarterback, many of them told me why they thought I was wrong. See, not everyone on the Vent is a sharp dude. Some of them just can't or won't see my genius, no matter how many times I point it out.

For April, May, June, July, and August I defended my Bank-On-It statement against the Mark-It-Down counter-attacks by my archrivals. I did this by reading between the lines of practice reports. Whenever you said something on the sports page, I showed how it supported my view. I also loaded my arguments with clever, genius-type insults to all those idiot, dumb-butt posters who challenged me. I told them but good. I used a thesaurus and you wouldn't believe some of the words I came up with.

And then you did it, Coach Richt. *You named the wrong quarterback*!

You completely undermined my Bank-on-it.

Don't you understand the position you're putting the Bank-On-It people in when you make the wrong decision? To you, it's just a career, but to people like me, it undermines the public acceptance of our genius on Internet forums.

I'll just come out and say it: It's disrespectful of smart guys everywhere. It's as if you care nothing for our Vent cred.

At this time, I would like to request a public apology and a full reversal of your depth chart decision at the quarterback position, and then we'll say no more about it. I've also attached my determination of who should start at the rest of the positions, as well as some plays I have made up that will go for touchdowns every time. Trust me. The halfback quadruple-reverse throwback hidden-ball goal-line sneak is a real doozy. You're welcome.

If you had not forced me into these demands, and had simply hit me up on Facebook once a week, you would be undefeated forever, just as I am on PlayStation. (I've tried out every one of my new plays there, by the way. If they work on a *computer*, for Spock's sake, you *know* they have to work on plain old grass!)

I would say more, but I am a busy fanboy. I have similar letters to write to the President of the United States, the Pope, and to Batman.

Fondly,

The Omniscient Fanboy

Richt's Reply to the Omniscient Fanboy

August, 2006

Dear Mr. Fanboy,
I am writing to apologize, in the realization that I have upset many of our most loyal fans. I've announced a quarterback depth chart differing from your preferences, and I know that's an occasion for deep grief and shame among the Bulldog faithful.

As I'm sure you're aware, it's our job as coaching staff to fulfill every dream of our fans at all times. But as I believe the great Abraham Lincoln once said, you can't please all the people all the time, except for Roe Dawg. (That last part was a joke. Ha ha! What, you think I don't read the Vent?)

All uproarious joshing aside, Mr. Fanboy, we have a very short window of time for setting our depth charts. Spring practice, Fall camp, decide.

For quarterbacks, we look at several things. How well have they absorbed the system? Do they have the physical tools? How quickly can they break the huddle, read the coverage, and get us into the right play? Then there are the intangibles: leadership, character, and—most crucial of all—Xbox simulation.

Not PlayStation, which you use, by the way. It is, like, so lame. ACC coaches and their fanboys, they're welcome to it.

PlayStation is so 2003. Mark it down. (Bank On It is lame, too, because it does not use my name.)

Our quarterback decisions nearly always come down to Xbox. We don't know what kind of quarterback we've got until the pixels are flashing, the simulated fans are cheering, and Mrs. Richt is bringing in a nice plate of peanut butter-almond cookies.

Mr. Fanboy, here's how it works: We get my defensive staff (WillyMart, Bagman, and Coach Fab) to play the part of the opposing team. Our offensive coaches are UGA, each one a potential quarterback. This year Bobo was Cox, I took Stafford, Callaway took Blake Barnes, and Dexter Dorcas IV took Joe T3.

See, Dexter is our intern, a computer science major who hooks us up with the Xbox. I can't ever figure out the plug thingy, but he's a whiz, knows every controller button.

We needed one more guy, so Dexter agreed to be JT3.

Funny thing is, on the practice field itself, Blake Barnes has been burning it up. Reminds me of Brad Johnson in beast mode. Kid pitches fireballs on missile trajectories, and he outruns our safeties. Kid is unstoppable—his only real problem is that Coach Callaway, who plays him on Xbox, isn't good with computers. He actually won't use the controller, but just shouts at the little quarterback on the screen, signals to it, that kind of thing. We try to help him, but he's old school.

Needless to say, the Xbox Blake doesn't do too well in simulation, and hurt the real kid's chances. Pity.

On the other hand, the intern Dexter is a techno-wizard. He has JT3 looking like Peyton Manning on steroids. Which is a thing, or so I hear. You didn't hear that from me. Don't mark it down, please.

As I said in the press conference, the QB rotation could change between now and midseason. I'm still trying to learn what all these buttons do on the controller. It's all way different from

Pacman and Donkey Kong, which we played back in the day. If there were more flaming barrels, I would rule.

But Dexter has virtual JT3 doing moves out of *The Matrix*, with slow-motion judo kicks in midair, taking out defensive ends as he soars ten feet high over the field. Now he has little death beams shooting out of his eyes, killing linebackers on the spot. Nothing lame about him, believe you me. JT3 is way ahead for starting against Western Kentucky on September 2.

Thanks for writing, Mr. Fanboy. I hope this gives you better insight into the intricacies of coaching.

Coach Richt

Ooga Quickie

November of Some Year or Other

Women and Children of Auburn!

Wail, moan, gnash your teeth, and cast yourselves from the toilet paper-laden branches of the trees of the jungle plain. Your words are as the feeble cheeping of the young chipmunk who is sectioned and sprinkled on the prophet's morning bran flakes. Your snivelings bring pain to the assparts of all worthy Dawgly peoples.

Your frail whimpering shall be silenced. Long and thorough shall be your thrashing by the spiked clubs of our warriors, that no spots be missed. Your few comely young cheer-wenches shall be divided and distributed as party favors among the dreaded fratboy tribes of primitive Milledge. Your firstborn male sons shall be given unto the she-warrior-priestess Yoculan and raised as boy gymnasts, who sow no seed, but frolic in the womanly worlds of interior decoration.

The elephantine ears of your chieftain, which flappeth in the wind like grandma's bloomers, shall be mounted upon the hallowed walls of Butts-Mehre, just above the water-fountain, and tobacco juice shall be spat into them by tourists unto the seventh generation.

Just a heads-up.

For Visiting Gamecocks: Hazardous
Conditions Warning

September 2007

Gamecock friends:
Having read your Internet forums for years, I've observed what your fans have said upon returning from Athens. Their accounts tend to read like a remake of *Night of the Living Dead* as performed by the cast of *The Andy Griffith Show*.

Like you, I'm sure, my Gamecock friends are exhilarated by the prospect of their team finally climbing to the pinnacle of tolerability after a century of play. They've never been to Sanford Stadium, and they want to know: Are all these stories true? Could

Georgia fans be as vicious, violent, and savage as the legends relate?

My answer to them is simple and blunt: Yes. It's all true.

Every blood-soaked word.

You may choose to believe me or not, but I've seen it all with my own eyes. One year, back during the Brad Scott Dynasty, I made the mistake of inviting a kindly, gentle South Carolina friend from our church. It was the sort of doomed endeavor you try only once.

We enjoyed our Saturday morning drive to Athens. First we talked over every highlight of Gamecock bowl history. Then, once we were out of the driveway and onto the road, we chatted about football and told jokes the rest of the way.

We pulled into our parking place in Athens, and I would estimate that my friend lasted ninety seconds after we climbed from the car. He was, of course, wearing one of those hats with an entire fake chicken dinner on the top, so he was quickly recognized by the unfortunate nature of his lifestyle choice.

It all happened in an instant. The mob descended, the men barking and the women howling. I recognized many of these predators as alumni of our top-rated law, journalism, and business schools. Chicken blood spattered on their expensive game day attire as they ripped my friend away from my protective arms, and spirited him away.

I tried hard to run after my friend, knowing his very life was in jeopardy, but it was a lost cause. Plus I didn't want to leave my tailgate alone—my favorite folding chair was in there. No one likes the tragic loss of a friend, even a South Carolina friend, but hey, life ain't perfect. I was already salting it away as a lesson to cherish, as I pulled out the cooler and the picnic spread. Live and learn. Thinking about it all helped me work up an appetite.

I thought about that last time my eyes locked with those of my former buddy. His eyes were wide as saucers, and I could read his lips: "HELP ME!" I never saw him again, though I did pick up a drumstick from his hat when I was tidying the tailgate site at the end of the day. His last effects, which I presented to his family. I let them know at church to take him off the attendance roll.

For the record, I'm told the Georgia enthusiasts probably took him to an immense bonfire over near our internationally-acclaimed veterinary science building. Lots of Gamecock fans went into that fire, or so I'm told. The part about roasting the grannies is a little shocking, I'll have to admit. But we take our football seriously in the Deep South. In a few more decades, my Gamecock friends, perhaps your children or grandchildren, will begin to understand. Depends on whether you ever make a major bowl.

I also saw what happened to some of the cars that bore Gamecock signs and bumper stickers. These were the antics of some wacky folks from our universally acclaimed chemistry and physics schools. (If you'd like more details on some of these academic highlights, I can get you a catalog or visit www.Uga.edu. This could be helpful if your school ever attempts to build its own world-class research university.)

As for the stadium experience, yes, those stories are true, too. Some scoff at what's been said about that upper deck we've built in recent years. Originally we called it the Tech Deck, but even Georgia Tech fans are smart enough not to sit up there. Fortunately, some other fan bases haven't figured it out yet, so we have some crazy, entertaining hijinks to watch during timeouts.

In short, we have a new tradition of throwing rival fans off the top row. I have a friend in the athletic department who swears there is a little team of janitors who run out at intervals and clean the mess off the sidewalks beneath that deck. Corpses are then recycled for educational purposes in our elite biological sciences research department. (Biology is the study of living organisms, in case you're curious.)

I can see how such things as the bonfire or the deck drops might detract from the idea of your coming to a Georgia game as a "family outing." Unless you prefer your family outings to be highly instructive and unforgettable for your children, who may or may not survive, depending upon their foot speed. Something like doing the old Lion Country Safari without the bus, much more educational.

Considering the pros and cons, I'd personally recommend that you and your other Gamecock chums stay home this Saturday. If you've already bought tickets, not to worry—I know a number of Dawg buddies who would love to take them off your hands. We'd like them at half-price or less, of course. You'll be out a few dollars. But you'd have your health, and that's all that counts, right?

Just meet us on the bridge for the transaction. We won't throw you off it. Trust us.

See you in Columbia next year!

Ooga vs. Kentucky, 2002

And lo, the great and invincible Empire of the Dawg, having whipped down the wimpian People of the Wine Coolers, known as Vandy, turned their eye northward, to the land of Tubby the Two-Timer, the site of the Last Stand of Curry the Unhirable, the place of they who call themselves Southerners yet liveth near OHIO; to the land where the grass is blue and the horses run feebly in circles, with dandified, jabbering midgets astride them, rather than manly fur-chested and shrieking warriors; where the deposed ruler known as the Monarch of Mumme, the Towel-Togged Tosspot, cheateth yet winneth not.

Yea, this is a land of unmanly feebleness where surely the men have besotted and stupified their minds with exceeding, abundant rivers of flowing bourbon.

And the People of the Blue Grass talketh of tearing down their girly-goalposts, for THEY have a wobbling wastrel warrior known as Jared the Gellatinous, the Jelloed J-Load, the Bluegrass Beacon of Bacon.

And what, they scoff, are the People of the DAWG to the Round Mound of Lexing-Town, the Pigskin Porker? For when he rolleth out, he really rolleth, and when he planteth his feet, the earth trembleth, and when he heaveth forth the ovoid, eagles fall lifeless from the sky.

Heareth the prophet, Blundering Blue Grass Blubber Grubbers! J-Load shall me mowed!

The Beacon of Bacon shall be shaken!

The Doughboy shall be rolled, cut up and cookiefied.

It has been said of olde that there is no blue food, but yea, verily, it shall be so. For Pollack the Pulverizer shall grab the pigskin, then skin the pig. Sullivan the Sackster shall bring forth the pain, Musa the Marauder will do fiendish things with One Thumb that Casey the Cowerer could not do with One Arm.

And One shall be the number of quarters that the People of the Dawg shall require to humiliate thee.

And Two shall be the number of blocked kicks.

And Three shall be the number of Dawgly quarterbacks who shall enter the fray.

And Four shall be the quarter when girly piccolo players from the Great Band of the Red Coats shall enter the game and prolong the pummeling of the pudgemeister.

And lo, even Loran of Dawglore shall come upon the field of battle and placeth his microphone wear the sun shineth not.

And Jared the Gellatinous shall be melted down to fat and grease, and flown forth across the sea by a fleet of jumbo jets, and poured out upon the entire nation of Iraq.

And there will be great howling and cries of surrender, but the Crisis of Crisco shall engulf all the nefarious nimrods there, and a great sizzling shall be heard.

And the land shall now be called Fry-raq.

And the incoming freshman class of North Avenue shall be decimated, and the world shall be joyful, and the BCS shall crown forth the People of the Dawg, and the Zookly Zig-Zaggers shall await their doom.

Amen.

Meanwhile, on North Avenue

Written after our victory over Florida, 2007.

November 2007

We need to take a short break from enjoying our win, and put in some quality time basking in the sheer misery of being a Georgia Tech fan.

It's a positive everyday habit, actually. You should do it no matter what, like brushing your teeth. But there are special moments for stopping to smell the roses. Or the North Avenue bus fumes. These are the times when Tech's misery and national humiliation are so spectacular, so Chantastic, they deserve our full attention. And they seem to come on Thursday nights.

Sure, the Dawgs have lost a couple of games. That's why watching Tech is good for the heart: It puts our little heartaches and ouchies in true perspective. Sort of like that old saying, "I felt bad about having no arms until I saw a man with no arms and no legs, and he also had zits, a really big nose, and a third eye." I may have gotten that saying wrong.

Thursday night: over the years, an evening for television comedy: *The Cosby Show, Cheers, The Office, Seinfeld*—classic shows all, but those were before Thursday night and the Atlantic Coast Conference came together for the perfect marriage. Funny, funny stuff. Like *Seinfeld*, a show about nothing.

And you can count on Georgia Tech to put in a side-splitting, pie-in-the-face, whoopee cushion performance at least once per year.

This Thursday night, quarterback Taylor Bennett, the heroic pigskin-slinger, had his coming out party. Only we're not sure what *kind* of coming out it was. A photo was displayed to millions of viewers, showing Taylor in his Halloween costume. That costume happened to be of a character called Tinky Winky, one of the Teletubbies.

"That's the one that has triangular antennae and wears a handbag," observed Chris Fowler.

Yep, he sad it. What, you didn't think the broadcasters were going to milk that cow for as many pails as possible? They showed the photo of the purple blob with the Tech face after every Tech miscue, referring to the offense being "led by Tinky Winky." Based on what the game offered, they had to find *something* to provide entertainment.

Bennett, the world's greatest quarterback when spotted 45 to 50 seconds to set up in the pocket (he'd be unstoppable in wheelchair football)—and a desperately leaping Calvin Johnson to throw to—had put up some big numbers previously: a gaudy 17 for 40 against the Virginia Unraveliers. (I said they were big numbers, not good numbers.)

By Thursday night, Tech had laid sole claim to the ACC Coastal cellar and was holding off anyone who wanted to climb down there with them. And for the ACC Coastal, the cellar is the most popular room in the house. But even in the division with Duke and UNC and UVA, it's only so big. Not everybody can fit. Virginia Tech made its bid for the attic, with a little help from Tech—and some hand-me-down clothing, too.

Yes sir, clothing! Before the game, four VT Hokies couldn't find their uniforms due to the standard campus vandalism. (We should have warned them.) Tech had nothing to do but offer their own road jerseys to the four players, including VT quarterback Sean Glennon. Glennon covered the "Yellow Jackets" lettering with black tape, then proceeded to run over, through, and around Georgia Tech's defense in the 27-3 rout.

To rub salt in the wound, Glennon mentioned after the game that Georgia Tech had been the last team he considered before committing to be a Hokie. Since he never became a Jacket, it was nice of GT to let him win a big victory in the gold and white anyway. It couldn't have happened if he'd been a Jacket himself.

Meanwhile, the long-suffering Tech fans were growing upset. Rather than descending into their usual downtown smog-choked stupor, they began throwing things on the field (presumably slide rules, Calculus texts, and action figures). And when Coach Chan Gailey's image flashed on the video board, nobody could hear his "drive safely" message because of the booing throughout the stadium—though the booing was a highlight of the evening, *any* kind of ovation being a rarity at Grant Field.

Talk to any Tech fan and he'll tell you about the advantages of "national exposure" attained when his team plays on an ESPN Thursday night matchup. Saturday-bound teams from elite conferences don't know what they're missing. Indeed, Tech was exposed nationally; perhaps it was indecent exposure.

Tech's Tinky Wink was certainly put on display. Bennett finished with four interceptions, by the way. "Teletubbies say, 'Eh oh!'" (That's some kind of catch phrase from the show. Don't stare at me like that—I Googled it.)

* * *

Keep in mind that five days previously, on a boring old Saturday, Georgia had gone down to Jacksonville and beaten the reigning national champion Gators, 42-30. It was an eye-opening game, just like Tech's. Except different.

Two weeks after that, Georgia blacked out its stadium before 93,000 in a momentous win over Auburn. Just like Taylor Bennett blacked out after being hit by a linebacker. Except different.

Georgia finished in a BCS bowl, ranked number two nationally. Tech finished, too. But different. They finished with a lopsided loss to Fresno State on a blue football field.

If Tech fans showed any signs of humanoid life or decency, we might actually begin to feel sorry for them after their years of untold suffering. We have a heart. We feel compassion for the suffering people groups of the world; Eskimos with melting igloos, that kind of thing.

But Tech people are an evil force. They owe a galactic-level debt to karma. I figure nine or ten more decades of suffering on their part, and I'll be satisfied. Or I'll let my great-grandchildren decide.

This is Tech. As my brother has observed, even their mothers don't like 'em. They'd stab your sweet little Aunt Emma Lou with their slide rules if they could.

At the end of the season, after the school's seventh straight loss to Georgia, Chan Gailey finally lost his job. It wasn't so much the rivalry thing; the engineers were worried about having to fix the video board in the stadium if people kept throwing things at it.

But you have to wonder who paid whom. The ex-Tech coach immediately got a Chantastic NFL job. For his family, the sun came out again for the first time in years. At Tech, the black, smoggy cloud continued to hang over the big, inflatable bee that UGA fans popped as a bi-annual tradition.

There would never again be a Night of Tinky Wink; a night of taking a beatdown at the hands of a guy wearing your own jersey. Our children and grandchildren will snort milk out of their nostrils over this one. The ACC: making family memories.

Ooga's List: Top Ten Reeking Hordes

10. HUNS: Germanic nomads, worthy and manly; skilled sackers of feeble villages.

9. THE SPANISH: Pillaged Mexico, looted ancient temples, reeked of onions; what's not to like?

8. HICKOLIAN HILL PEOPLE: Relentlessly feeble-minded, cleverly wear blinding colors in battle, constantly rebuilding fallen empire, brick by brick. Need to rebuild stadium first.

7. (tie) STAKE-DRIVING HORDES OF VLAD THE IMPALER and INTERNAL REVENUE SERVICE: Impalers or Gougers? Ooga say, matter of taste.

5. GREEKS: Hid inside giant horse, then enslaved academia through fraternities; Ooga gotta respect that.

4. MONGOLS: Never bathed. Shrieked incessantly. Cool mustaches. Forerunners of grunge rockers.

3. (tie) YANKEEISH CARPETBAGGERS and RAIDING, PILLAGING VIKING PEOPLE: Yankees more evil, Vikings had cooler hats.

1. TIGER WAR EAGLE CHEETAHS OF JUNGLE PLAINS: Very confused about horde name, very feeble, annually overdue for epic beatdown.

Ooga vs. Florida, 2002

The prophet got this one wrong, but let's not quibble over details.

Behold, hear ye well this Declaration of Dawgly Domination, all ye lands! Give forth thy tributes of sullen, submissive surrender. Send forth thy sacrifices of fine, plump possums, goats, and tender woodchucks for the great Dinner Pail of the Dawg. Send forth thy gifts of various and sundry bodacious cheer-virgins for the prophet's Party Palace of Dawgly Disco.

Prepare ye a way to the Dome, which shall be rife with Dawgliness, barbarian brazen barking, wild and warlike woofity-woofing, and rude and rowdy ruff-ruff-ruffing.

One Hundred is the sum of points inflicted in the previous two weeks of brutish Dawgly beatings, and One Thousand is the number of years the Dawgs shall reign, and One Hundred Thousand is the number of the People of the Dawg which shall descend upon Alt.Hell Stadium, for One is the number of battles the Dawgly Warriors must win to claim their rightful legacy as Dawgly Dictators of the Eastern Waste.

And lo, here stands the Big Dawg, shining in glory, for his many wimpish and womanly whiplings, do they not lie at his feet?

Here be the Chickenly Chuckleheads, the dunderheads of doofus-ish delusion.

Here lie the Tidish Tuska-losers, probation their prickly prize.

Here lie the Hickolian Hill People, the reeking orange hordes of Fulmer the Foul and Casey the Half-Shouldered and Double-Mouthed, the cellar their destination.

And here lie the Enfeebled Bottom-Feeders, the Vandyish and Kentuckian tribes, though they, too, shall surely taste victory over the Hellbound Hill People.

All are our slaves. And yet, what heareth the excellent, hair-tipped ears of the prophet? Boasting from the Mouthly People of the Gator? They who know the pain of LSU's foot far up the hidden havens of their hindquarters? They who have tasted defeat at the unmanly hands of Old Mist?

The Gator, is he not a creature of five teeny weeny little limbs, the most dominant being attached to its hindquarters, and one flapping, mammoth mouthly orifice? Yea, Spurrier the Spurious, the Visered Vizier, has he not skedaddled forth to the reeking hordes of the NFL? Are they not led by Zook the Zero, he of the Zucchini Brain?

Let it be proclaimed forth that Rex the Regurgitator shall scramble forth in panic, one painful step slower than Pollack the Pulverizer. The People of the Dawg shall open a Great Can of Jonathan upon him, and he shall be buried deep within the bowels of the earth, and of Boss the Brutal. Gilbert the Goremeister shall bring forth the Industrial Sized Pail of Pain, and distribute forth generous servings.

And the Greene Machine and the Shock Jocks shall invade forth the End Zones, and pitch their tents there, and accumulate many points in honor of Damian the Deadly, who giveth of himself in battle, and who is greatly to be honored among all the People of the Dawg.

And once again the barking of victory shall resound at the Cocktail Party, and no more shall the People of the Gator steal forth glory from their superiors, who have enslaved them through all the aeons of history.

And the People of the Dawg shall continue their march to worldwide Dawgly Domination.

Amen.

Don't Run Down Clemson

January 2008

We were recruiting one those big offensive tackles we always need. He was named A. J. Harmon. This mammoth kid was a blue-chip athlete, could be a blocker or a tackler, and his decision was coming down to the wire. Everybody wanted A. J. Harmon, and the Dawgs were trending upward.

Then he gave an interview. He said Georgia was really stockpiling the talent. UGA was going to be a "monster," he said. He also knew that Rodney Garner was putting lots of defensive linemen in the NFL. Having said all that, Harmon had to admit: "Clemson is a great place to play, and I love the idea of running down the hill."

DAMN. Running down the hill. How could we compete with that?

Clemson has always recruited well. It's set in a bustling corner of South Carolina—well, no; I've been there myself, and never seen any actual bustling in progress. At any rate, Clemson is a geographical wonderland, second only to Candyland, the board game.

For one thing, there's a *lake*. Auburn doesn't have a lake. Athens doesn't have a lake—sure, there's Lake Oconee, but it's a whole hour away. Clemson has a lake *right there*. You can walk by it, or just stand and look at it, or contribute by taking a leak in it. Your choice.

But the clincher, of course, is a *hill*. Clemson has a lake. And they have a hill.

So what, you say; Athens has a *lot* of hills. Fully-functioning hills, complete with uphill and downhill functions. Some of these have been called *rolling* hills. Our hills roll. They rock!

But wait a minute. Clemson's hill is *right there next to the football field*. It's not a rolling hill at all. In fact, it's technically probably a *hillock*, according to my dictionary. Maybe a hefty mound or a semi-knoll. *Roll* is something Auburn fans do to their tree.

Still, there's something magical about this hillock. There must be, because Brent Musberger is *astounded* by it. Every time the announcer visits and beholds the sheer pageantry of that hill and the young men scampering down it, the adjectives burst from him like a verbal geyser. Assistants have to wipe the exclamation points from his chin.

But A. J. Harmon said it best when he stated, "I love the idea of running down the hill."

However, the non-bustling folk of the lower piedmont didn't stop there. They have a lake. They have a hill. And they have a *rock*. I wasn't exaggerating when I told you this was a geographical wonderland. Don't even get Brent Musberger started when it comes to the rock. It would concern his doctors.

Yes, it's true that nearly every school in America has at least a few rocks scattered around campus (even the FCS schools probably have their pebbles). Note that Tennessee has built its entire football identity as "Rocky Top." They want everyone to know they are the rockiest of all tops, absolute tops when it comes to rockiness. Who could be surprised they recruit so well?

But even the Volunteers don't have *Howard's* Rock. That's the Clemson rock that sits on the Clemson hillock not far from the Clemson lake.

This superb specimen of stone formerly belonged to Frank Howard, iconic head coach at Clemson for many decades. He wasn't much of a coach, as iconic head coaches go, but he did get the Tigers to six whole bowls in some thirty years—the kind of wild success that used to drive Gamecock fans insane. And the legend goes that he had a rock that he used as a doorstop. This is a matter of true football lore; I've done my research here.

One of Howard's buddies had given him the rock as a gift, supposedly because he picked it up in Death Valley, California, right out of the dust and probably beside an old beer can. And Clemson has a Death Valley, too, one of a great many parallels between Clemson and California. Lakes and hillocks are over there, too. The stuff in the gift shop was way overpriced, so a pet rock was a sensible souvenir. Also, the rock bore an unmistakable likeness to Howard's bald, weather-worn noggin. See, look at this. ☞

L-R *Howard's Rock; Howard*

For years this honorable piece of gray flint, from the Sedimentary family of California, faithfully kept Howard's office door open. It allowed for a breeze, prevented stuffiness— actually it performed helpful rock-type services, compared to the business of sitting quietly in a glass case, as they ultimately prevailed upon it to do.

But when the coach was doing some house-cleaning in 1966, he told another booster, and I quote, "Take this rock and throw it over the fence or out in the ditch . . . Do something with it, but get it out of my office." Again, I'd never make this stuff up.

It wasn't an iconic coach speech to compare with, say, a Lombardi or a Bryant, a Rockne or a Holtzzssh. But for the fervent

Clemson Tiger, these are hallowed words. Try this. Walk up to any Clemson fan, say, "Take this rock and throw it over the fence," and he will solemnly take your hand, a small tear will form in his eye, and he will complete your statement: "Do something with it, but get it out of my office!" Then protocol dictates that he has to buy you a beer or perform a feat of heroic service. The two of you might even run down a hillock together.

The rest, my friend, is history. Howard handed the rock to a booster, who thenceforth placed it on a little pedestal in the end zone, where it could watch the football games up close with its little rock eyes. The next few seasons, the Tigers won anywhere from three to six games per year, so it was clear that the deep magic of the rock and the hill conspired toward greatness.

But wait, there's more. We haven't even discussed the *rubbing*. Almost immediately, players began to assemble at the top of the hill, rub the rock—perhaps understandably mistaking it for Coach Howard—then barrel down the hill screeching like little girls. Normally there is no screeching in football, but an exception is made when there's pageantry.

In 1970, new coach Hootie Ingram ("They're not saying 'booty,' they're saying Hootie!"—Brent Musberger) arrived on the scene at Clemson, ushering in futuristic new ideas about the game. It was his belief that players should run onto the field from the *west* rather than the east.

Since it didn't occur to anybody that the rock and its little home could be moved to the other side as well, the rock had to watch the team entrance forlornly, from one hundred yards away. And rocks don't have sharp vision like, say, hawks or trees.

The rock was deserted. There was no rubbing. The whole experiment was a disaster, the Tigers going 6-9 in home games during these years, and a mutinous team demanded a return to the hill, the rubbing, and the shrieking scamper down the slope. Or at least a good downhill bustle.

Hootie's booty was relieved of duty.

The team still went 2-9 and 3-8 for a couple of years, but dang it, that wasn't the point—there was rubbing and running, just as God intended when he made football.

That's why, decades later, Georgia was still struggling to recruit against Clemson. Prospects would come to Athens to see SEC Championship banners, Herschel's Heisman, luxurious athletic apartments, an elite NFL draft record, and a fatherly head coach.

To which Clemson could say, "Son, how would you like to rub a rock. To run down a hill?"

Clearly it was a stand-off. If you don't get this, you're not up with the times. You need to take off your red and black glasses and think like the Young Men of Today. They like hip hop. They're into computer games and social media. And they're crazy about rock-rubbing and running down the hill.

As it turned out, A. J. Harmon became a Dawg. He signed a grant-in-aid to come to Georgia, citing the rumors that Tommy Bowden could be fired at Clemson. Think about that. Harmon had no idea whether some new coach would come in and have the team enter from a different side—or God forbid, even replace the rock with one that looked nothing like Howard's scalp, and didn't feel as good to rub! The lake, the hill, the rock: these were wondrous things, but could they be counted on?

Somehow we won the battle with Harmon, but it was a close call. On the eve of Signing Day, a recruiter from Auburn came to his home and said, "Son, how would you like to throw toilet paper all over a tree?"

An Ooga Thanksgiving

Furman Bisher used to do these, but in language only a century less archaic than Ooga's.

And Lo, Ooga giveth thanks unto the Big Dawg for *many* things, yea, verily:

For the foul and reeking minions of the Hickolian Hill People, enchained in slavery, their orange apparel running red with the blood of Dawgly vengeance.

For goodly, polished iron spikes, sharpened for battle, mounted upon the White Stripe of Helmetly Righteousness, and dipped in the poison of Dawgly vengeance.

For comely hordes of fine young cheer-wenches, capable of worthy feats of gymnastiness, divided thusly into two factions; one yelling, "Oo!" and the other, "GA!"

For firstborn male puplings, ready to be trained in the Warlike Way of the Dawg, upon the gift of their first spiked club and the trophy ear of a vanquished Hickolian.

For an orgy of swinely Thanksgiving feasting: possum-ka-bob; tasty squirrel cutlets stuffed with savory vegetables and live insects; and yea, pickled Techling pie with loads o' whipped cream.

For the slow, painful deaths by prolonged pain of all of the

Nattering Nimrods of NATS fanboy nation, lo, all seven of them, and to the glorious music of their weeping.

For the Pilgrims and the Indians, and the savage combat with which they smote one another and devoured each other's remains for The First Thanksgiving, as in the story which all young warriors are taught.

For a well-woven and comfy loincloth, which chafeth not in the manly places.

For two days after Thanksgiving, when the warrior awaketh from the orgy of turkeyish feasting, and enjoying leftovers combed from one's manly tuft of facial hair and heated up in the microwave.

For possum-ka-bob. What, hath Ooga already mentioned it? Mmm, possum-ka-bob.

Ooga vs. Auburn, 2002

For this memorable week, when Venters were recovering from Jacksonville grief while fraying at the seams over possibly clinching the SEC East for the first time, Ooga received a special request. Someone on the Vent wanted his thoughts on Robert Baker, the Auburn receiver who taunted Uga, the mascot, in 1996 and had a narrow scrape with becoming a soprano. Here he is known as the White Powder Man, a reference to certain legal problems that ensued for the player in question.

From olden days riseth the legend of the White Powder Man, he of the Tiger Eagles from the Jungle Plain who catcheth passes and selleth evil opium to children, like unto the thuggish Auburnian ones of olde. And in the ancient time of 1996, the White Powder Man conspireth to enter into the holy and forbidden place, the Dawgly End Zone, which is a transgression punishable by the instant and toothly deprival of manliness.

And the White Powder Man believeth not the warnings, and approacheth the End Zone, where dwelleth the sacred dawg named Uga. And being foolish and unbrainly, he taunteth the Great Dawg, and the sacred dawg entereth the White Powder Man's End Zone promptly, teeth bared, and removeth said manliness so that the White Powder Man needeth much of his own sniffly snortation forthwith.

And it is said that the only white line he crosseth that day was the one which entereth his nostrils. But the People of the

Dawg riseth up and entereth the Tiger Eagle End Zone repeatedly, even unto four overtimes, and great was the rejoicing among men of good dawgliness.

And lo, the ancient tale is told again, to all young Tiger Eagles who cherisheth their budding manliness and wouldst not have it removed by toothly caninish surgery. For the Tiger Eagles of the Jungle Plains, they who changeth their heads and symbols like unto Pez containers, are an arrogant and taunting people.

They are the people of Dye the Drunkenly and Tater Tot the Tiny, yet they are arrogant and taunting.

They are the people owned forth in slavery by the Tuscaloosish Tide People, yet they are arrogant and taunting.

They are the people who throweth toilet tissue in the trees of Toomer's Corner and calleth it manly and tribely, yet they are arrogant and taunting.

Hear, O Pezzly War/Tiger/Eagles of the Village/Jungle/Plains, thy End Zone shall be desecrated once again by Musa the Marauder and the artillery of the Greene Machine. Thy womanly quarterbacks shall disappear forth in a steaming pile of Pollackipation. Even the biceps of Itty Bitty Billy Bennett the Bootmaster shall prove too powerful for thy maidenly feebleness.

Yea, beat thy chests, taunt forth, bringeth forth the smackliness, and feed lustily on thy confidence from thy wimpish victory over Lousy Anna Monroe, for the People of the Dawg are One People under One name, not Schizoidish Pezzly dispensers of the White Power Man's candy. We are Dawgly Warriors. We seek forth the rightful throne of the home in the Dome, which we maketh our own.

And merciless shall be thy treatment, for the Loveliest Village/Jungle/Plains shall become a field of slaughter. And the head of Richt the Righteous shall be anointed with Gatorade, and he shall be carried upon the shoulders of the victorious warriors to the presence of Tommy Twerp-ear-ville the Talkmaster, he who proclaimeth championships and delivereth not.

And Richt the Righteous shall reach forward with manly hands and rip off the great flapping ears of the Talkmaster, and hold them aloft, even as a trophy. And they shall be shredded and sprinkled over the great Alpo feast of Dawgly Uga, as seasoning. And this shall be an act of mercy, for then the Earless Talkmaster shall heareth not the endless whining of they who boast in season and whimper off-season, even the Pez People.

And the People of the Dawg shall travel to the Dome of the Dominant, even in their SUVs, even in their RVs, even upon foot, in a great triumphal parade. And the Big Dawg shall lift forth his leg and mark his new territory, and await the feebleness of westernly challenge.

Amen.

Certificate of Ownership

Anytime. Every time.

I am UGA, and I carry Tech around in a tiny cage that I keep in my pocket. When I go to parties, I pull out the little cage so everyone can laugh at the miserable bug whimpering inside it.

Sometimes I take it out and smush it into yellow goo with a football. Sometimes I smush it with a basketball, sometimes with a baseball. Doesn't matter whether I use a tiddly wink—it's really fun to smush. And the best thing about the scrawny little bug in the cage is that it's constantly re-smushable, like a cartoon character, and it weeps and whines just as much every time I smush it. I love owning Georgia Tech.

If Abraham Lincoln were still around, he might find the UGA fanbase in violation of the Emancipation Proclamation. We have branded the Arch on that yellow butt. We have placed their little pencil-thin legs into teeny, tiny little shackles.

My friends, Georgia Tech is a fully owned subsidiary of the University of Georgia Athletic Department.

If Georgia Tech were an island, it would have a big UGA flag impaling it, right in the middle, and Michael Adams would already be setting up a bogus research facility on it.

If Georgia Tech were a song, our head coach would get a nice check in the mail whenever it was played.

If Georgia Tech ever gets misplaced, it will end up in the Lost and Found bin, and you and I can just walk up and say, "That ugly, reeking, lying and cheating thing belongs to me, thank you very much. I OWN IT." Not that anybody else would want it. We just like owning it.

As a UGA fan, I deducted Tech from my taxes last year. About seven of every eight years, I pay no taxes. If I were only renting Tech, I couldn't do that. Fact is, I OWN TECH. YOU DO TOO. When I get hungry, I go over and raid Paul Johnson's refrigerator. Amazing how many Twinkies he keeps on hand. I don't know their basketball coach personally, but I can tell you he's over here at my place right now, cleaning the gutters. After that, he's going to grout my bathroom tile, and he's going to smile and tell me he likes it.

He has to, because I own him. I own them all, even that little twerp reading his advanced quantum physics textbook all by himself, in the upper deck of my stadium on North Avenue in Atlanta, during what passes for a football game there.

Saturday is more than a game. It's about who runs this state, and that means it's about ownership. Today I'm spiffing up my teeny, tiny cage. I hosed it down, washed away all the yellow goo. And I've got my football ready.

Greenbacks for Cam

With Apologies to Dr. Seuss

In 2010, a shocking theory circulated. It was whispered abroad and on Paul Finebaum local affiliates that maybe Cam Newton didn't choose Auburn simply for the joys of toilet-papering trees. Say it ain't so!

Some speculated that, shocking as it may have seemed, Auburn had remunerated its pet Camster in fiscal units amounting to, oh, about $180,000, either because of its generosity toward a ramshackle church Daddy Cecil pastored, or maybe with the idea of having Cam lead them to a national championship. One of those two, anyway.

Discussion ensued. Much discussion. Any minute now, the hammer was going to fall, if the Vent or Tiger Droppings, the elegantly named LSU site, were to be believed. It was Auburn fans against the world, a phenomenon that occurs in nature only every six weeks or so.

All these details of bagmen and laundered casino chips were hard for your child to follow, leave alone the typical Auburn fan (always a good policy, leaving them alone). Neither My Weekly Reader *or* Highlights for Children *even covered the story.*

The simple of heart and mind needed the Cam Newton NCAA controversy explained to them as it would be set forth in a kid-friendly book like, say, Green Eggs and Ham *by Dr. Seuss. So here's how Dr. Seuss would explain the Cam-troversy of 2010.*

As you can imagine, Bama fans liked this one.

December 2010

GREENBACKS FOR CAM

I am Cam!
Cam I am!
Cam don't have no
greenbacks. Damn!
"Did you take them,
Cam-I-am?
Did you take
Greenbacks for
Cam?"
I did not take them!
Cam-I-am!
I did not take
Greenbacks for Cam.
"Did you take them

Here or there?"
I would not take them
here or there.
I would not take them
anywhere.
I did not take
Greenbacks for Cam.
I did not take them.
Cam-I-am!
"Did you take them
On the Plain?
Did you take them
From Jimmy Rane?"
I did not take them
On the Plain.
I did not take them
From Jimmy Rane.
I did not take
Greenbacks for Cam.
I did not take them!
Cam-I-am!
"Did you take from
Lowder? Dye?
Or AU's rich alumni?"
Not from Lowder.
Not from Dye.
Nor AU's rich alumni.
Not from Rane
Or on the Plain.
No dough did Cam-I-
am obtain!
I did not take them.
Cam-I-am!

I did not take those
greenbacks.
Damn!
"You did not take
them.
So you say.
But *Cecil*.
Did *he* make them pay?"
Cecil? Yes! It's like you say!
Reverend Cecil made them pay!
Reverend Cecil ran the scam.
He passed the plate for Cam-I-am.
He took from Lowder.
And from Dye.
From AU's rich alumni.
He took from Rane
Out on the Plain.
Two hundred thou! Let's have champagne!
Cecil ran the pay-for-play.
And Cam knew nothing. Zip. No way.
He's cool with NC Double-A.
I am Cam. Cam I am!
Bring my Heisman.
What a sham.

Ooga vs. Georgia Tech, 2002

November 2002

Behold the hordes who dwell across the land, and beateth upon their chests, and screameth savagely, and smiteth one another, and trampleth the entrails of their brother-hordes into the earth, and breaketh wind when and where they feeleth like it. Are they not proud hordes, the People of the Gator, and the Tiger Eagles of the Jungle Plain, and even the fallen Hickolian Hill People who settleth for the bowls of the half-hindquartered?

But the manliest and greatest among all the tribes are the People of the Dawg; and the feeblest among them by far are the Nattering Nimrods of NATS, the weasels of whinish whimpery, the Arch-Nerds of the Pimply-Wimpiverse.

For into battle they do not run but skip, and they do not bellow but giggle, and their heads are not spiked like true warriors but Spock-eared, and they hath beaten their swords into slide rules.

And lo, about them there are told One Thousand Feeble Fables, and the Nattering Nimrods are symbolized by the wily coyote which chaseth the road runner in vain. For the coyote is mangy and starving and unworthy, and it dwelleth in a desert of despair, like unto Dudd-Grunt Stadium, whereas the road runner, like the People of the Dawg, sprinteth by, on its way from glory-era to glory-era.

And the coyote thinketh himself an engineer, and he fashioneth many wimpish ACME devices by which to capture the road runner, but in the end he plummeteth off the cliff, or weareth the crispy face of scorching, or findeth himself crushed under the boulder of bulldoggery. And the road runner hurrieth on to his championship game, while the coyote is made sport of by the world's mocking laughter.

And the Nattering Nimrods, being pimply and wimply, wail and whine and gnash their teeth, and the People of the Dawg haunteth the Nerdly Noggins of the Nimrods three hundred and sixty-five days and four seasons and countless moons, knowing their gigglesome giddiness and Tickle Pilish Poindexterishness shall always render them as the wretched rejects of their own chosen region.

And lo, their cheer-wenches are frat pledges in mascara.

And their color glorifieth the tee-tee of terminal illness.

And their emblem is that of a despised garden pest.

And their girlish warriors loseth in battle, even unto Wimply Wake Forest.

And their recruiting hath been cast out into the darkest and most desolate reaches of New Jersey.

And within a generation, these Nimrods shall have perished from the earth, for their seed is unmanly and populateth the earth only with sickly sucklings.

But the People of the Dawg shall speed them along in their reeking elimination from the bowels of the earth, for there shall be a rambling reckoning in the Sacred Sanctuary of Sanford, where dwell the Holy Hedges of Herschel. For lo, these are Dawgs of Destiny, Hounds of Heaven, Canines of Conquest.

In the Dusk of Tuscaloosa prevaileth they; in the Tumult of Tigertown prevaileth they; to the Dome of Dawgly Domination shalt they travel; and the pimply pestilence of the poltroons shall not deny them. For Richt the Righteous shall lead an onslaught of Dawgish Doom, and the brittle bones of the Bilbovians shall be shattered and ground into the earth, where even the buried ashes of Grizzard the Greatheart shall stifle them.

Even Lewis's ashes will give them an ash-kicking.

And as the entrails of the Nattering Nimrods are like unto manure, great shall be their fertilization of the Holy Hedges, which springeth up from the blood of the vanquished from generation to generation. And in this way, and only this way, shalt the feeble Techmites provide their seed to the future, for their feeble foibles are at an end, and their stadium shall be steamrolled and converted to an Infertility Clinic as a memorial to their unmanliness; whereas the People of the Dawg shall dwell in the House of the BCS forever, and getteth the best wenches, and enjoyeth the finest craft-grogs in kegs that never runneth dry. Amen.

Fresh Air for Olde Mist

This was written before the hammer came down. Ole Miss had some oopsies. They failed to make crime pay. Then, just before I published this thing, Ole Miss was freed of Freeze. See what I did there? See what Freeze did there?

January, 2016

Ole Miss has rebranded itself. Just like that thing Coke did in the 80s, with New Coke and Classic.

This New Coke, we were told, was going to be incredible. We all ran to the grocery store to pick up a carton of the beverage the day it came out. But it tasted like—well, frankly, it tasted like Pepsi. Forget this sludge. We wanted our "Old Coke," soon to be known as Coke Classic. The company responded. Then, gradually, "Coke Classic" was just Coke again.

Ole Miss Classic was as reliable as a bottle of your favorite soft drink—a consistent product year after year. Sure, occasionally an Eli Manning came along, and there might be a big season— maybe even a mindboggling ten wins. Hey, that was okay. You knew the next season, they'd be back to three or four wins, and the planets would be spinning in balance again.

But now, forget all that. It's a brave new world in Oxford. This is New Ole Miss. Accept no substitutes.

Ole Miss kicks SEC butt. It's as though the South has risen again, this time with a few extra Stonewall Jacksons. Suddenly,

Alabama—at the peak of its own powers, mind you—is not casually strolling down Highway 78 and taking the pick of the litter. That new Bama-B-Gone spray is working pretty well for Ole Miss. So does the LSU Tiger Repellent and the Malzahn Zapper. Kids are picking up the Ole Miss cap on ESPN signing announcements. The guy with the mike says, "Wait, do you want to do that again? I think you accidentally picked up the Ole Miss cap."

"No sir," says the kid, who grew up on the streets of inner city Chicago. "It's always been my dream to play for the Rebel Bears." In the 2013 class, recruits hailed from Illinois, Georgia, Florida, Texas, and, Australia.

Wait, what? Did you say Australia? Where the toilets flush backwards?

Yes, on the other side of the world, a kid stood up, said, "Bye, mate," to his pet kangaroo, and sought his fortune in the place they dream about in the land down under: north central Mississippi. As a matter of fact, from every corner, recruits are deciding they want to cast their lot with the Magnolia State.

It was as if you and I took a nap and somebody warped the known rules of the universe while we were asleep, just a wee bit.

Naturally, when coal turns to a diamond in the space of one year, the whispering begins. Mischief! Monkey business! At the very least, roguish chicanery!

Come on, folks, don't overthink it. Surely you don't think anything improper could be going on in SEC Western Division recruiting. This is the Bible Belt, and you should be ashamed of yourself for even considering something so unwholesome.

Sure, Ole Miss blowing up in recruiting was about as likely as Switzerland invading China. But I'm here to set your mind at ease. There are entirely logical reasons to account for the whiplash emergence of Ole Miss. It all makes absolute, perfect sense, and this is your notice to settle in for the Hugh Freeze Dynasty of college football. Nick Saban? Urban Meyer? Craven poltroons, stumbling milksops by comparison.

 Let's start our journey of discovery with the personal brilliance and irresistible appeal of that very head coach. His dynamic personality is a magnet for gifted athletes. And it's clear that his former nests, Lambuth University and Arkansas State, are high-tech factories for coaching brilliance. More a legend than a man, Hugh Freeze has given us every reason to expect he'd show up in Oxford in 2012 and quickly destroy all SEC competition.

Not only that, those of you with your minds soaking in the sewage of nefarious recruiting speculation haven't taken into consideration the lure of Ole Miss itself. I'm somewhat of an authority on The Young People of Today, many of whom are more often than not on my lawn, digging through my petunias to fetch their baseball. These youngsters are a new breed. They love their tattoos and piercings, their rap music, and the later novels of William Faulkner and Eudora Welty—both lifelong Mississippians.

Who else in college football can compete with the opportunity to play a stone's throw away from the very spot where *The Sound and the Fury* was written? Many a fistfight breaks out on the practice fields of today as blue-chip prospects argue over the symbolism in Faulkner's Snopes trilogy.

Or maybe your typical kid from South Florida or downtown Atlanta longs for the progressive urban life of North Central Mississippi. Several new stop-lights have been installed, and there's a new Tastee-Freez rumored to be on the way.

We need to come to terms with the fact that millennial kids across America and Australia have their hearts set on being a Rebel Black Bear for life. They've grown up watching Ole Miss perform in all those SEC Championship Games in the Georgia Dome. What's that? You say Ole Miss last won an SEC championship within a few days of JFK's assassination, and has never played in the Dome?

Whatever. Leave it to you to bring up nit-picky trivia.

Whatever the explanation, Ole Miss's recruits are real and they're spectacular. In the first week in February, a killer class is as natural as Groundhog Day. Except the Groundhogs wake up, come out of their holes, and say, "I know I committed to another school, but suddenly I want to go to Ole Miss."

Not only that, but there's this cool thing where a lot of their friends follow them, getting scholarships of their own at the school, even though they're not athletes at all! Or even "college material."

I've heard of cases where players' parents happened to get nice jobs in Oxford right around the exact time their kids chose that school. You tell me that's not the work of the Good Lord. I know a lot of my friends said that when they heard. "Good Lord!"

It's heartwarming to see how the Rebel Black Bears believe in the traditional family and in having old friends around us, so that they don't just recruit an offensive tackle, they recruit the whole community around him and the pavement under his feet. And when he gets to Oxford, he finds nice cars might be waiting for him, and grades might be a lot easier than he expected, and classes much fewer. Ole Miss is awesome, and all of this is paying off as we see future outstanding citizens being molded for life, wholesome, All-American young men such as the Nkemdiche brothers.

The success of "New Ole Miss" is a story of redemption. It tells us that sometimes, if you're sick of being the little guy, if you dedicate yourself to greatness, if you believe hard enough, and if you're hooked up with one or two rich boosters who love spreading happiness and goodwill, you, too, can go to the head of the recruiting class.

Ooga vs. the Georgia Dome, 2002

Behold, the prophet bringeth forth this, the ultimate pronouncement of Dawgly Glory, over a tasty chipmunk-and-bacon omelette braised with fresh yellow jacket honey. But lo, thou asketh, "How cometh yellow jacket honey to thy table of manly gorging? For even I, a foolish and gigglesome youth, know yellow jackets are not bees, and giveth no honey!"

And the prophet replieth forth to say, "Pound thou the yellow jackets 51 times and they giveth honey, grape jam, or whatever thou ask of them."

For the bodacious can of whoopassishness hath been fully and justly opened upon the Nattering Nimrods of North Avenue, and wimply is their whining, wussish is their whimpering, and womanly is their weeping and wailing.

But the People of the Dawg listeneth not, nor addeth they even one Nimrod moment to the Holy Highlight Tape, for the Day of Dawgly Domely Dominance beckons. It has been decreed even from ancient times, that the Swinely, Swaggering Sweathawgs riseth up from the wallowsome muckish mire of mediocrity to challenge they whose rightful crown waiteth in the Dome of Doom, yea, even the People of the Pig, led by Lord Numb Nutt, he who bringeth forth the miracle of losing to Kentucky in his own Hawgly Home.

But the Piggly Wigglies hath no worthy heritage among they who do battle in the Southeastern Fields of Slaughter, for they are Swinish Switchers and Swappers of their conferencely allegiance, having crept in from the abomination and desecration of the Southwesterly Tribes. And Lou Holtzheimer, too, cometh from the People of the Pig. And Danny Fraud, the Dithering Doofus of Death Valley, leadeth the People of the Pig, though it bringeth shame even to a pig. And lo, they loseth to the Citadel, yea, even in recent times.

Turneth back, Piggly Punkish Porkpackers! Thy bacon shall be quakin'. And thy ham shall be sandwiched between slices of Boss Bread, with Pickled Pollack and manlynaisse. For pigs walloweth not on artificial turf, but only in the mud of thy reeking region of wretchedness. This is the Day of the Dawg, prophesied forth for two decades, when the great coronation shall come upon the head of Richt the Righteous, and they anointeth his head with a big fat raise, and his incentive clause runneth over.

And great shall be the barking of the People of the Dawg, and the Houndly Howling shall raise the roof of the Dome of Dawgly Domination, and the Great Red Sea shall overflow from the Havens of Cheap-seatly Hunkering, and the hymn shall flow forth in great melody: "Lo, it's Great to Be a Georgia Bulldawg, It's Great to Feast Upon the Splattering Entrails of the Vanquished!" ...What, thou knoweth not that one? Lifteth thine eyes to the Great Jumbotron of Joy, and singeth thy praises. For the Day of Atonement hath arrived, and long shalt be the Reign of the People of the Dawg, and non-existent shall be their mercy, and many shall be the legions of comely cheerwenches, and Larry Munson shall liveth to be the age of two hundred seventy-nine.

Amen.

Ooga's Kirbaic Prophecy

Hard to believe eleven years passed between the last Ooga prophecy and this one.

Christmas 2015

nd lo, even as the prophets of antiquity telleth us:

> *BEHOLD, Cease forth the whining of the feeble and undawgly. For a Deliverer shall surely come. He shall descend from the highest heavenly expanses of the West, where dwelleth the crystal trophy of empire. And he shall walk and coach and holdeth press conferences among us. Though snuff shalt he dippeth not, nor have any filthy habit. Though a little social drinking forth is no big deal, as sayeth the Methodists and Visigoths. Anyway, For ten years shalt he labor among the Tidish People, and then shalt he be worthy to lead the PEOPLE OF THE DAWG.*

Yea and Egad and Forsooth and Shazam, it cometh true. Thus it came to pass that KIRBY THE CONQUEROR cometh forth from

TUSK-A-LOATHA, after the time of the holy press release of tidings of great joy, and an end to the curse of not showing up for the really big battles. The deliverer cometh, forsaking the crimson and hounds tooth in favor of the Tooth of the True Hound of Junkyard Legend; and forsaking the beehive hairdos of the trollish women of ALADAMBAMA, and the Bear tattoos of full-body anointment, which are ugier than OOGA THE PROPHET'S southern exposure.

And he taketh upon himself the mantle of Dawgliness, even the threads of red and black, and no polyester, yea, and all manner of Nike gear, and RECRUITETH FORTH! HELL YEAH, HOW HE RECRUITETH, sayeth the prophets and soothsayers and bloggers, yea, and even those who just moved here and don't follow it too closely and are really mostly NFL guys and are also into hockey.

MIGHTILY did Kirby the Conqueror recruit, even unto three thousand miles, across the fields of wheat and the misty mountains of preppy ski people recruited he them, until he reached the GUNSLINGER OF SKINNINESS and even the ROAD GRADERS OF GREAT GIRTH, even Big Country who chaweth tobacky indeed: and Kirby consumeth rib-eyes among them in the president's box, yea, RARE UNTO BLOODY consumeth he his steak thereon, and slayeth the cow himself, and flasheth forth the championship rings of supremacy, and chooseth he a coordinator also of great girth and tricky formations, and yea, a bad-ass commander of the front lines, who blocketh and seweth the field with the blood of those who rush the passer. Hallelujah.

AND THEN, LO, having accomplished these things, he speaketh forth words of the oracle and Advanced Coachspeak, and giveth high fives all around, and ascendeth again into the West, while his disciples beheld, saying unto them, and to his assistant coaches thereon, "My time has not yet come, for I have business with the Father, even Lord Saban, and one more ring sucketh not.

"But go ye unto all Athens, unto all Georgia, and unto the uttermost parts of the earth, recruiting forth, and saying that the Day of the Dawg draweth near. Go ye unto all the five stars, and even unto the four stars, they of positions of need, and lo, a three-star or two who cruiseth under the radar, but sheweth out in camps; why not?

"Even so, hunker forth on the FIVE STARS, boys; yea, verily, owneth forth the nastiest and most dreaded of the youngish and still zit-besotted warriors. Even unto the tenth graders, goeth! And unto the ninth graders, goeth!

"And unto the fifth graders, if they killeth it in Pee Wee Ball, go forth and eat Happy Meals and trade Pokemon cards with them and even unto their Cub Scout meetings goeth! Lo, whatever it takes. For behold, I ain't lyin'. Recruiteth from the womb of the young maiden, just breaketh no laws and it shall be fine.

"Teach them," sayeth he, "and proclaim the truth of Dawgliness, and baptize them in the spittle and holy drool of the BIG DOG. For I am coming again, yea, as the trumpet soundeth from the corner of the SOUTH STANDS, I will ascend to Athens once more, upon the dawning of the new year, when the season of the pigskin dieth out and the treachery of the winter season, that is, ICE HOCKEY, shall be upon us, to weeping and wailing and consuming of adult beverages.

"And then," sayeth the Kirbinator, for yes, he is still talking, and is long-winded, and his Uber runneth late, "shall I burneth my tacky crimson shorts and houndstooth gear. GLORY! And BARK, I shall, on all fours. And give press conferences aplenty, and trouble the dreams of Jeff Schultz. And LORD SABAN, he will henceforth become LURID SATAN unto me.

"And this shall be a sign unto you: I shall TWITTER FORTH messages of good tidings among you, and work the phones, and do mighty signs and wonders, assembling forth my STAFF, and talkin' the talk, and just being awesome.

"And upon this Butts-Mehre I will build my kingdom. Though I don't get the name. Couldn't they have called it the Dawg House or something? Amen!"

A Visit from St. Nick

For the 2016 season, Radi asked me to write a column after each game. These could be any kind of column, just so they offered a fan's perspective of the game. For most of the games, I was able to find something to write. Toward midseason, when things went pretty far south, it became, let's say, a bit of a challenge. Here's the column for the game in the Georgia Dome against North Carolina, Kirby Smart's debut.

Twas the night before football, and all that. Whatever. Rewrite the thing yourself, subbing football stuff for visions of sugarplums and all that rot. Knock yourself out.

See, last season didn't leave me with any poetry in my soul, you dig me? We couldn't score on Georgia friggin' Southern. UGA-Missouri was an epic battle of the big toes of scrawny kickers. Ragweed sprouted in the end zone. The zero on the home side of the scoreboard was finally painted on, because why waste pixels?

No offense, but it was that kind of season: um, no offense. So I tried to enter 2016 with realistic expectations. A first down here or there would be nice.

So Ma in her kerchief And I in my UGA cap, had just settled down by the TV—oh, snap. I said I wasn't going to do that.

Anyway, we turned on the game and Georgia elected to receive. Say WHAT? We actually *wanted* our offense on the field? Fire Kirby!

Then, on the first play, we ripped off a really nice run, and then another one. With a lumbering tailback so lively and quick, we knew in a moment it must be St. Nick.

Oops. Sorry. Then, of course, Lambert took a couple of sacks. Yep. Okay, it was nice while it lasted. But the defense held, we got the ball back, and Lambert hit a really nice pass. And as I drew in my head, and was turning around, o'er the goalline St. Nicholas came with a bound.

"A touchdown!" I exclaimed. "I remember these! You get six points, right?" And the Tiny Herschel in my head replied, "Yep. But guess what? Sometimes you even get two or three or four of these touchdowns in one game."

I said, "In your dreams, Tiny Herschel. You should probably quit and send me one of your other personalities. Like Despairing Realist Herschel."

But he said, "Look at my man Nick. Did you already forget number 27?" So I did look. He was dressed all in red, from his head to his shoes, and his clothes were all tarnish'd with linebacker ooze.

I'll admit it. As another touchdown transpired before my very eyes, I was starting to feel the poetry. "Look, honey!" I said. "Herrien B Carryin'!"

"Is that a rapper name or what?" she asked. But by then, before I could go on the Internet to see if Herrien was by some chance from Darien, Chubb was back in the game. However, things had gotten tense. We had a tiny lead in the fourth quarter, and we weren't too good at holding onto these leads. I thought of Tennessee last season. However, Chubb spoke not a word, but went straight to his work, and he shut up Fedora, that UNC jerk.

He broke a long, nasty touchdown run! We were going to beat a ranked team, instead of *being* a rank team. I leapt to my feet and began exclaiming sonnets and rhyming couplets as I watched Chubb trot off the field, having inflicted 222 nasty yards on those who aspired to tackle him. I called upon the spirits of Keats, Wordsworth, and the gal from Nantucket.

But poetry failed me. "Never sub for Chubb!" I shouted, and my wife groaned. The cat gave me a dirty look. So I gave up on verse and commenced speaking in tongues.

But I heard him exclaim, as he jogged out of sight, "Happy Chubmas to all, and to all a good night!"

How'd You Like a Nicholls Sandwich?

Week One was a piece o' cake—with extra icing; an exciting victory everybody was jazzed about. Week Two: uh oh. A wildly forgettable performance against a team nobody had heard of. I decided to tell the story of a typical family suffering through that game.

Get the picture. All decked out in red, you're on the driveway.

"On Our Way to See the Bulldogs Play!" Junior reads. "Can I stick the sign on the car, Dad? Can I?"

You smile and nod as you affix the two UGA flags to the hood of the family roadster, the Chubbmobile. Your wife emerges from the house with a handful of luscious pigmeat, soon to be sizzling at your tailgate somewhere on the fourth level of the Hull Street parking tower.

Junior says, "Eason for Heisman! Eason for Heisman!"

"Wrong, son!" you reply, ruffling his hair. "Chubb for Heisman. Eason in '17!" and you bump knuckles.

The weather is heaven-like. This is it—the day you've been waiting for through the nasty, unrelenting seasons of hockey and strange new Olympic competitions. Georgia football has a home game.

The first stop is MeeMaw's, to drop off the baby. "Here are some extra Pampers, and, oh, I almost forgot her toys," your wife says. "She usually naps just after lunch, which will give you a chance to watch the game."

"What game?" asks MeeMaw.

"Traffic isn't getting any thinner," you say, glancing at the time on your phone.

"Chubb goes back. Chubb throws it a mile!" says Junior, acting everything out. You say, "Chubb runs it. He doesn't throw it. Buckle up, son. Let's do this thing."

"Hit a home run," says MeeMaw, holding up the baby's hand to wave.

Traffic is bad, but who cares? You're listening to the hymns of sacred Dawgology—the Munson tapes. "Why is Oscar the Grouch talking about the Dawgs?" asks Junior. "Did they really stomp on somebody's faces and rip out somebody's heart?"

Your wife smiles and begins telling him all the legends of Larry Munson. Life is good.

At the game, you talk to Bertha May and Big Ookie, the nice couple who sit right behind you, catching up on the last few months. Bertha May shows your wife her surgical scar. Then the band is on the field. It's time for the video and the Spell Georgia cheer. "Who is Nickles?" asks Junior.

"DAWG FOOD! That's who they are," you say, and you high-five and bump knuckles. "Knuckles for Nickles!" you say. *Genius.* Probably the best joke you've ever made. "Dad, you're as awesome as Eason," your son says, and a little tear almost escapes your eye. Almost. "As awesome as Eason. Not quite as awesome as Chubb," you say. And you're about to have some more male-bonding fist-bumps, but the kickoff happens.

Eason hits Godwin for 36! Chubb barges into the end zone! Everybody hugs everybody. Even Big Ookie's hunting buddy gets into it. He holds onto your wife about five seconds too long. But you can't think about that right now. The Dawgs are on defense—and Briscoe intercepts! Hugs all around. "I love you, Dad!" says Junior, but you glance elsewhere, a bit uneasy. "Let's switch places," you say to your wife, detaching her from Big Ookie's hunting buddy.

Then there's an odd play—twilight zone stuff—where Nicholls drops Chubb—CHUBB—for a five-yard loss. Just a freak thing. No way that would happen again in a million seasons.

Then Eason throws an incompletion. "Dad?" asks Junior uncertainly. "Honey?" asks your wife. Big Ookie drops his first F-bomb of the season.

"It's fine!" you bark, and soon after there is a missed field goal. "Can I have ice cream?" asks Junior, losing interest.

"NO!" you thunder, way too loud. "I mean: no," you say, but it's too late. You've done it now. Junior's lower lip begins to quiver. Old ladies, seemingly hundreds of them from distant sections, including a few nuns, are turning and staring at you. That lady over there isn't calling DFCS, is she?

You catch the evil eye from your wife, who is soothing your distraught son. Who has time for this nonsense? Nicholls is driving down the field, dammit! Six plays. Touchdown. Chaos! We're through the looking glass—a riddle wrapped in an enigma wrapped in a tortilla, or something like that. Up is down, wrong is right, Nicholls scored on us.

"What is HAPPENNINGGG?" wails Big Ookie, throwing his hands into the air. You stand up and cuss Kirby and the horse he rode in on, then sit sullenly through halftime. Your angry wife has stalked off to take Junior to the concessions stand.

You realize Bertha May has been telling you something about her enlarged goiter for the entirety of halftime, and is waiting for some kind of response. You mumble, "Yes ma'am. Sounds awful." She gasps and harumphs, turning away.

The second half has started. *Nicholls has driven 75 yards for a touchdown.* What fresh hell is this? In a flash of philosophical insight, you find yourself reflecting that, you know, football has an unhealthy priority in your life. You need to look into other hobbies. Stamp collecting seems like a path to explore. You've always wanted to read the world's great literary classics. This season held such a promise, but . . .

Then Isaiah McKenzie breaks a long one, and you're shreiking like a little girl for your Dawgs. Vaguely you realize it's the fourth quarter and your wife and son are still missing.

The game is almost over. Irrationality has reasserted itself as Georgia clings to a two-point lead against a squad of friggin' liberal arts semi-athletes from a school you've never heard of. Big Ookie's hunting friend slides into the seat next to you, and you realize he's been missing for a while, too.

"She really loves you, you know," he says, gently placing a hand on your shoulder. "She has things she's always wanted to say to you, and before she comes back, she wants me to share a few of them with you." You take a swing at him, a roundhouse knuckle sandwich. He ducks, and your fist collides with Bertha May's recently dentally-enhanced jaw. Big Ookie yelps, then leaps at you.

And that's the last thing you remember. Until you wake up in the back seat of your car. Your wife is driving. Junior peeks over the front seat, cotton candy sticking to every part of his face, and says, "Best game ever. I hear next week is Misery."

"Missouri," you say, whistling through a gap in your teeth.

"You never know," says your wife.

Next Week Is Misery

Last week's Nicholls column ended with your little kid saying, "Next week is Misery." For a good while Saturday night, I thought the little guy had nailed it.

But after his dad corrected him with "Missouri," Mom said, "You never know," and as usual, Mom had the last word. When you watch these Dawgs—you never know.

The symbol of this team is IMac. Is he going to put the ball down late in the fourth quarter, inviting a loss against one of the lesser FCS teams—or is he going to put the team on his tiny but twisty IMac shoulders, roll through the end zone, and show this ain't misery, it's just Missouri? IMac giveth, IMac taketh away.

Sure, if our offensive line were the Grand Coulee Dam, Eason and Chubb would have been washed deep into Canada by halftime. The Royal Canadian Mounties would still be leading search parties.

AND if our defensive backs were a deportation force, there would be hordes of illegals running free through the Southwest—though our guys did snag three nifty interceptions.

AND when our placekickers teed it up, folks on every side of the field ducked under their seats. The best you could say about special teams was that we've brought suspense and chills back to the extra point.

As for Eason, he was all over the place, too. He threw That Pick, the one you've known all along was coming. The one that was Freshman Stafford's favorite toss, sometimes two, three per game.

The one that was bound to come on the road, at the worst possible time. That Pick finally happened, and it was somewhat like the strict Presbyterian who tripped down a long flight of stairs, woke up in the hospital, and said, "I'm glad I got that over with." So are we. We'll give you that one, Jacob.

But you know that other one, that final pass of the night? Circle that one. It's a keeper. We'll be wanting more of those, lots more.

Because that's the only one we're going to remember after this game is erased from the DVR. Eason missed some throws, but when it was fourth and the full ten and whole game, when he really truly absolutely positively had to come through, HE DID. Mackenzie was rolling across the end zone like a tumbling tumbleweed, with a Missouri DB on him like cling-wrap, BUT IMAC HELD ON.

The matchup was Chubb versus the front seven, sometimes the front nine of Missouri, so it was another less-than-Chubbly evening. But on that final now-or-never drive, Sony Michel picked him up with a terrific run.

And put this on top of your brain and tape it down good. Who scored the winning point? MR. HAM. The kicker no one's too sure about. As we say on the Vent, Bake Ham for Missouri.

Our defensive backs had some oopsy moments, but on their final play, with disaster two first downs away, they jarred the ball loose and fell on it.

The point is, Brent Musberger was ready to light his cigar and celebrate the pageanty of it all for the zillionth time. We were looking done for; we had a lot of things that had to be done right, from a lot of people—some of them unlikely—and on every single one of those suckers, MISSION ACCOMPLISHED. Eason. Michel. IMac. Ham. DBs. Head coach.

My question is this: Can you have the proverbial Buy-In-Moment against unranked Missouri? Does it have to come in a place like Knoxville, against a Top Ten squad, and does Larry Munson have to be present to put it into crazy-old-guy slam poetry?

Because I've had my questions about this team and its buy-in. We don't have a lot of seniors; do we have team leaders? We have a brand new QB again, a Bama loan at nickle back, a rent-a-tackle from up north. Not much emotion along the bench, with most of the electricity on the sidelines generated by staff, not players. We saw an end-zone celebration, but not like the one in Tuscaloosa in overtime in '07.

Because that was Tuscaloosa. And that was Saban's first year—he had his own buy-in to figure out. But wherever you are, whoever you're playing, there has to come that moment when staff and team bond, where emotion becomes organic rather than fake juice; where 85 or so students and a few old guys with clipboards become fused into a distinct and indivisible unity called TEAM.

Thus, like that kid asked his dad on the way home: Are we there yet?

Ole Mist: A View from the Ledge

Shell-shocked superfan, I'm lookin' at you. Right there out the window of the high-rise, with your beer-stained lucky UGA cap sideways on your head, those bulging, bloodshot eyes, and the shattered remains of a TV remote in your hand. Move over, I'm climbing out to join you.

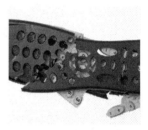

In Memoriam: AT&T TV Remote (2013-2016)

"Oh, hey, Sax. Watch the pigeon poop," you say. "It'll mess up your pants."

"I already messed 'em up Saturday. What day is it? I guess I should change clothes. To be honest, I haven't felt like doing much of anything."

"Right there with ya, Sax. It's kind of peaceful up here, though. Folks look like little bugs down in the street. Like I could step on 'em. If I could see what colors they were wearing."

"Yeah, this is nice. Can't even hear the UT Vol War Cry of Adequacy up here. Butch has finally got 'em to the dizzy heights of adequacy, and they want the world to know it. Say, I have to ask. We're not doing, like anything crazy from this ledge, right? You've got a lovely wife and kids to think about."

"I'm lookin' at em. They're down there yelling, 'Jump! Jump!'"

"Point taken. Mine aren't too happy with me, either. Fifty-inch screens don't patch up too good, do they? Now my wife can't see HGTV, and I'm sleeping on the sofa."

"Same here. Stuck my big ol' foot through my Samsung. Like Munson said, some property's gonna be destroyed tonight. I done my share, dang it."

"Not sure that's what he meant. But listen, are we hoisting the white flag for this team? I mean, it's still September."

"Depends on injuries. Are the defensive backs still healthy?"

"Perfect health."

"Damn it."

"Point taken again. Still, you know, we gotta give the new staff time. Rome wasn't built in a day."

"But it was sacked and stomped on and pooped all over and laid waste and filled with tattoo parlors and used car lots by uneducated savages in a day. History repeats itself, don't it?"

"That's unfair. For one thing, the barbarians ran a much cleaner program than Ole Miss. But also, the Romans had no kind of decent quarterback. We've got one who's just having the light come on."

"I'm afraid the Vols are going to shut it off again. Which is probably for the best. I'm hidin' my eyes as it is."

"Might as well, while your TV is smoking. Listen, I can see I'm not cheering you up. I don't guess there's any sense asking you to climb back through the window with me."

"Nah. Besides, they've got one of those big nets for me to jump into down there. See it? I've always wanted to do that."

"Wow. I do see it, and I still think you should climb through the window with me."

"How come?"

"Those are some of our receivers holding the net. You do the math."

Tennessee: Guy Walks Into a Bar

Another hangover-experience column. In a wild game, Georgia seemed to win with almost no time on the clock on a heroic touchdown pass—only to see Tennessee hit a Hail Mary with :01 left. Let me entertain you.

Okay, I got one, fellas. Stop me if you've heard it before. Goes like this.

Three guys walk into a bar. No. no, make it four guys. Right? Four guys walk into a bar. They all step up and try to order their drinks at the same time, they're talkin' over each other, then they stop and look at each other. Who has the right of way?

Bartender, he's seen this one before. He laughs and says, "Okay, order in the court. Which one of you guys goes first?"

First guy says, "Well, I should, because I've spent my life shrouded in gloom. I am a philosopher, you see. And my specialty is the bleak, unceasing despair of the human condition. I've traveled the world and interviewed the saddest, most pessimistic human beings on the planet, for whatever the reason may be for their cosmic angst. I'm the worldwide expert on suffering, my friends, and it stands to reason that, seeing what I've seen, no one suffers more than me. Therefore I should go first."

Bartender nods respectfully and says, "Fair enough. Whattaya have?"

But just like that, the second guy interrupts. He says, "Not so fast, my friend. I'm a film director, which may sound glamorous to you, but my gig is to direct all those sad animal commercials. You know the ones I mean? That chick sings, "In the Arms of an Angel," and shows whimpering puppies and kitties and stuff? You see one of those occasionally, for thirty seconds. I'm filming and editing those spots sixty hours a week, my friends. Looking at sad animals. Hearing that song over and over. When I close my eyes at night, I dream about whining cocker spaniels at night. I think I deserve the first drink."

Bartender gazes at him in awe. "My gosh, that's awful," he says, and Guy Number One, even he steps back respectfully. But before that drink can be served to Number Two, the third guy pipes up. What's he gonna say? "Hold up, men. I teach violin lessons to little kids. Eighty hours a week I listen to eight year olds trying to pluck a violin string. Think about that. We live next door to a really smelly paper mill. In a tiny apartment. Me and my wife Phyllis from Mulga, famed telephone personality from Finebaum's Show. Who demands lovin' every night. I am a man of constant sorrow, folks, and the least you happy-go-lucky partakers of sunshine and lollipops can do is step out of my way so I can get down to some serious alcoholism."

At that, of course, the whole bar grows silent, until the fourth guy steps up. No way he's topping that last one, right?

"Big Dawg fan," he says.

And the bartender pulls a sawed-off shotgun from behind the bar, grabs his box of ammo, and says, "Outta my bar in the thirty seconds it takes me to lock and load, you SICK FREAK. This establishment is for victims—not masochists."

That's all I got today, folks.

Generic Gamecocks Column,

Insert Taunt Here

The hurricane winds descended on Columbia last week and did $50 million worth of improvements. Thanks, folks! I'm here all week.

What, you've heard that one? Please understand, I'm in trouble here—it's a Gamecock game. These things are UGLY, unless, say, the air wizard Grayson Lambert is there to set an all-time NCAA record. (It happened.)

Other years, not so much.

Yesterday wasn't the kind of stirring, operatic victory it's easy to write about.

I've always called Columbia a little taste of New Jersey in the Deep South. It's just kind of there, because it has to be somewhere. The laws of spatial physics require it. The University of South Carolina is a century-plus study of how not to do college football. Begin with the genius who decided to use a chicken as a mascot. Just the image to strike fear in the hearts of, say, the Presbyterian Blue Hose. A flightless barnyard bird whose life is spent functioning as a cheap alarm clock in the morning, peck-fight sporting events for rednecks in the afternoon, and the Colonel's dinner bucket at night (which, of course, is why South Carolina actually loses regularly to Kentucky).

You want more? Not enough chicken-trolling for ya? Well, the idea was to call their stadium the Cock Pit, but we all know it looks more like a cockroach that has expired on your basement floor; those girders thrusting into the air, simulating the lifeless legs. Traditions consist of a "fight song" called "Step to the Rear" which is actually a failed Broadway show tune dating all the way back to 1967. The musical was called "How Now, Dow Jones."

I'm betting you didn't know that. You're welcome.

The lyrics of the "fight song" begin, "Would everyone here kindly step to the rear?" Before and after 1967, South Carolina and its fans have kindly (sometimes unkindly) stepped to the rear more times than any of us can count. Last year's 3-win season offered an opportunity to step to the rear nine times, with the bonus of a Hall of Fame head coach doing so himself mid-season.

A better choice of bird would have been the swan, because Columbia was the swan song for over-the-hill championship coaches ready to curl up on the basement floor of college football, thrusting their clipboards and athletic shoes skyward before heading to that great after-game press conference in the sky. Paul

Dietzel, Lou Holtz, and Spurrier all won national championships before stepping to the rear, a rear end that was not a rare end.

And Spurrier was, by every measure, a rear end, surely tops in the chicken pecking order, as well as being one of the great peckers in the game in other ways. Before he arrived on the lowest of the low country fence post to crow the dawning of a new day for Carolina, the chickens averaged about a bowl for every decade or two, about like eclipses but less common than locust plagues. However, there were bowls aplenty under Spurrier, and even one golden appearance in the Dome, though it ended in yet another bucket dinner for Cam Newton (56-17). Awwwwwk! Buck, buck buck.

No champions were available this coach-hiring go-around, but the next best thing was: a guy with "champ" in his name, which at least makes for good bumper stickers. Will Muschamp, or Muschicken, as I'm henceforth deciding he'll be known, has one other good trait. He's long-time buddies with Kirby Smart. And, see, Kirby didn't want to show up his buddy, so he told Jacob Eason to go Easy-On his friend. (See what I did there? Words are fun!)

This is absolutely why Eason went 2 for 57 or something like that, and I defy you to prove otherwise. I win. Only problem was that Nick Chubb laughed when asked to do the same thing.

Recruiting lore says that Chubb made campus visits in Columbia twice, and Spurrier wasn't there to wow him. This was the third time, and Spurrier still wasn't there. Neither was the rushing defense. Or any semblance of an offense. They had all stepped to the rear.

Let the record show that Columbia got off relatively cheaply from Matthew, both hurricane and last-decade quarterback, but Chubb and his leather-totin' friends did another several million dollars worth of improvements. What, you've heard that one? Up in the first paragraph? How was I to know you'd still be reading this thing? It's your life, dude.

Nerd-Whipped

You again? Yeah, you, the unsinkable Dawg fan. It's Saturday in Athens (which is beginning to sound more like a threat than a promise). You and the boy, you're up to the challenge.

"Are you sure you wouldn't rather go with me to look at the leaves in North Georgia?" asks your wife.

"You serious, woman? When's the last time I missed a home game?"

"Well, just remember what portion of a plow-mule's anatomy you made out of yourself a few weeks back. Big Ookie and Bertha May are our friends. They have sat behind us in the stadium since late-era Goff, and you punched poor Bertha May in the jaw. Big Ookie may never forgive you."

"Come on, honey. That was totally an accident. Besides, it wasn't like I hit him personally, you know? Just his wife. Guys are cool with this stuff; I forgave Big Ookie at the end of that LSU game a couple of years ago, when we won the sucker, and he peed himself in excitement, and it got on me."

"That's different. You guys pee yourselves two or three times a season. Toss sweep goes for twenty yards, you men pee yourselves. But I had to bake six casseroles to get back in Bertha May's good graces. She *drank* 'em through a straw, even the brisket. Plus I had to stay and hear the blow-by-blow on her latest surgeries. Just behave yourself, all right?"

So now you make your way up Aisle 330. Junior trails behind, citing rushing stats from last week's South Carolina victory. Soon your backseat neighbors arrive; Big Ookie and Bertha May. Bertha May is sporting a huge white brace over her jaw. A young guy is with them, too. With that jaw brace, Bertha May kind of favors Flatfoot Frankie Sinkwich back in '41, when he beat Florida almost single-handedly with a broken jaw.

"Dad . . ." says Junior, standing and pointing.

"I know," you growl softly. "Don't stare at it."

Then, louder, you say, "Hey, Ook! How's it hangin', man?" You jump up and extend your hand, but he only nods cooly, acknowledging your presence.

"Wezzat pooty wiiife o'yord?" emits Bertha May, grabbing and smothering Junior in a hug. Dang, now the boy's going to smell like—well, like Bertha May. Some kind of *Ew de Tropical Rain Forest* fragrance. You'll have to hose him off after you get home.

"That pretty wife of mine is looking at the leaves and flea marketing and buying apple cider, lady-crud like that," you reply with a neighborly smile. She nods enthusiastically, which causes her jaw brace to go *squeak-squeak-squeak*.

Big Ookie whispers to her—he's not speaking to you directly, and she's speaking lockjaw. "Ookie wants-oo meet nephoo." So that's who the other dude is. Ookie's nephew.

"Snively Cadmium IV," says the young man, stepping toward you and offering a squishy hand. "Freshman at Vanderbilt."

Red alert! Today's opponent! Come on, man.

Ookie knows it's uncool to bring an enemy to our section, unless you've captured them at the tailgate by yourself, and you've got 'em hog-tied and gagged. Consorting with the opponent is stadium treason.

But for some reason people do it, just about every week, and it's annoying. The Auburn ones are too stupid to understand your taunts. The Tech ones giggle and shake their pom poms in your face until you get up by a few touchdowns. Then you look up and they're just gone. You never actually see Tech people leave. My theory is they Sneak out during the hamburger game up on the matrix, during the Big Reveal, like the weasels they are.

Then again, this is just a Vandy fan. Bringing a Vandy fan, or a directional school fan, if those exist, is probably more a misdemeanor than a crime. What can go wrong with a Vandy fan?

But how does one *talk* to one of those? It's something you've never attempted. You ask, "Whatcha studyin' up there?"

"Russian Literature, Post-Turgenev," he smiles. You nod, open your mouth, and absolutely nothing comes out. You can only turn around and take a seat.

But no problem. They're teeing up for the kickoff, and the Dawgs are about to pound these grey poupon-panty-waisted, tea-and-scones-snorting, pinky-up quiche-eaters. It will get ugly fast. Our rushing game is no longer a game, since last week. It's a land-based assault. There will be little Chubb-marks all over these guys for life, and everyone will point at them at their opera house and laugh.

Vandy receives. A tackler whiffs. Another tackler whiffs. Nine more red jerseys run around in random directions, like those old buzzing electric football games, and finally Reggie Davis pulls the Vandy guy down at your four-friggin'-yard line.

"Whooo! Whoo!" calls out Snively, leaping to his feet. "Vandy candy! Vandy CANDY!" You turn and stare. No way they really say that. Come on, man.

Still, you're not too worried. It's four yards to the end zone, and Vandy has, like, three yards of offense for the whole season. Plus—yes! A hanky on the field! Maybe there was a block in the—

"Offsides on the kickoff," says Mr. Ref. "Kicking team. Half the distance."

Okay, it's not funny anymore. No more fooling around, Kirby. Release the Hounds.

Before a play even happens: "Another penalty, defense," says Mr. Ref. "Just because. Half the distance."

Ball on the one. Still, it takes Vandy two plays to score. It's probably their second longest drive of the year. "Woo HOOOO!" chortles Snively. And he actually begins to sing their fight song, in a robust counter-tenor:

Dynamite! Dynamite! When Vandy starts to fight!

Down the field, with blood to yield . . .

Everyone in the section is staring, mouths agape. Who knew Vandy had a fight song? Big Ookie has pulled his shirt up over his face.

You're a little annoyed now, because, of course, there goes the shutout. You turn around and say to Mr. Cadmium IV, "Just so you know, you and your kind, you're about to be introduced to one Mr. Nicholas Chubb."

"The Chubbinator," adds Junior.

"Yeah, the Chubbinator," you say, giving him a fist-pump. It sounds lame, but you and the kid need a united front. Later, you'll work with him on proper trash talk.

Nicholas Chubb goes for three yards on two carries.

"That punter," says the Vandy kid, "I assume this is your Mr. Chubb?"

Now you're thinking, Big Ookie is behind this. Yeah, that's the ticket. It's a big conspiracy. The miserable SOB brought this kid just to get your goat. Probably hired him off Craig's List, under Vandy Nerd for Lease. What other job could a lit major get, other than hire himself out to annoy people?

You shoot an evil eye at the whole crew of them, but all you see is Big Ookie holding a nacho while Bertha May sucks off the

Cheez Whiz with a straw. You make a mental note not to look again. Maybe ever.

As the game goes on, and Vandy still leads, the student gets to use all his cheers. One of them goes, "Ha-RASS them, Ha-RASS them! Make them relinquish the ball!"

The next thing you know, it's the end of the game, Georgia is actually going for it in desperation, and your vicious ground assault is fought off by guys from a land-locked state who, for unknown reasons, go by an Anchor Down theme.

It's a friggin' nightmare. You've been nerd-whipped. Taken a beating at the hands of the little kid down the street who has asthma and takes violin lessons.

"This was invigorating," says Snively as you leave the stadium. "I must try another game of this Foot Ball soon. With whom do your boys play next week?"

"BYE," you mumble.

"No need to be sensitive," says the Vandy dude. "We can't all be good at these gentlemanly sporting exhibitions."

Auburn: Banana Republic

A group of researchers put a chimpanzee in a little room. The chimp would sit in a chair, facing a handle in the wall.

When he pulled the handle, a tray would slide out holding a delicious banana. He'd gobble it down with joy, then, when he became hungry again, he'd pull the handle once more—and yes! Another banana would arrive.

The chimp would be thinking, "This is the life. Primate Nirvana; I've got it made." The little stomach would rumble, he'd pull the handle, claim his ripe, yellow Chiquita, and grin at the world with those amazing teeth.

Until about the tenth time he pulled the handle.

That's when a roaring gorilla would crash through a door, slap the chimp in the face three times, pick him up, and throw him around the room like the suitcase in the old Samsonite luggage commercial.

The alpha monkey would depart, and the poor chimp would lick his wounds, peel himself off the wall, and struggle back to his chair.

After that, he'd look at the handle longingly, but he'd resist pulling it until he was absolutely starving. Maybe that last thing was a fluke. Finally he'd tap the handle just with his pinky, and the door would explode forth, the gorilla would barge in again, dribble the screeching chimp on the floor, use him as a handball, and leave.

Then the chimp would be taken to his cage, whimpering.

The next day, all of this would happen again. Ten bananas, two beatings. After a while, it simply defined his life.

Scientists undertook this fascinating study as an attempt to understand the mysterious psychology of the Auburn fan.

It makes sense. Like our friends from the jungle, Auburn fans are entertaining at times. They can be cute when you dress them up in their colors. Some can even ride bicycles and smoke cigars. But they also hiss, show their teeth at you, and screech, so you should watch yourself unless they're behind bars, which often happens.

Try and understand. What's it like to have a pretty good season, convince yourself you're on the juicy fruit train, then finish every single friggin' year getting slapped around by the two big alphas, the only two rivals that count?

Your Auburn friend is that chimpanzee, and Georgia and Alabama are his personal gorillas. That's life.

This is why your AU fan is just a little neurotic, nervous, and jumpy, has facial tics, and very occasionally throws his poo at you, either online or otherwise.

War Eagle, baby. You can actually hit it big one season (2010), but even then, as you smoke your victory banana, you can't really, truly enjoy it. Next year, you know that gorilla's waiting. He's cracking his knuckles, waiting for you right now.

No wonder these people are off kilter. The scientists have given up trying to understand the toilet paper on the tree thing, but they know it's a deeply psychotic manifestation of something or other. Something anal-retentive, obviously. Throwing their poo at the tree might violate a public ordinance, so they must make— well, do.

And why else would you have two different animal mascots, and two clashing colors? (Blue, cool and calm; orange, advanced dementia)

So this year, why were we surprised when it happened again? You didn't think it would, neither did they, but this thing is bigger than the both of us. Auburn came into Athens with a Top

Ten ranking and a six-game winning streak. Boy, was there going to be some sweet, sweet Tiger Eagle revenge!

I mean, last year they somehow got beaten in their own place by a Chubbless Dawg team, a struggling Lambert, and a dysfunctional coaching staff apparently communicating with each other through the water-boy (who wasn't taking sides).

Yet they couldn't beat THAT Georgia team.

This year? Get serious. UGA had lost four out of six, including Vandy; been beaten down by an Ole Miss team that earlier had been one more fat banana for the Bluish-Orange Tiger War Eagles from the Loveliest Village/Plain/Swamp. *UGA had no offensive line.* Auburn had the four horsemen of the AU-pocalypse for its defensive line. UGA had an inaccurate, true freshman quarterback.

This would be an epic beat-down, tying the all-time series once again, setting up the Iron Bowl Game of the Century.

Except it wasn't. It didn't. Auburn fans loaded their jaw with chaw, stocked up on potty tissue, pulled the lever—and the gorilla came out.

And damned if this time the gorilla wasn't a little fella with a moustache and coke bottle specs, his head trapped in a helmet so that he showers and socializes with it on, and he did it all with his toes!

Plus Mo Smith, he was good too, but Rodrigo is more fun to talk about.

Dial up 911 on your cell, Auburn. Emergency line. Get it? 9/11, the UGA-Auburn record lately; two bananas in more than a decade. In one fell swoop, the Gus Bus has another flat tire, and the Kirby Smart Cart may finally start.

As usual, two or three thousand manly, star-studded and stud-started recruits saw it all. Some of them, some good ones, will still choose the genetic insanity of the Auburn "family"—they always, always do, because of the bananas offered—but it won't matter.

This is one monkey those guys can't get off their back.

Advanced Philosophy: The Tornado Game

Through the history of thinking men, certain questions have troubled the souls of every generation:

- Is there a God?
- Why is there pain and suffering?
- What is the meaning of life?
- Georgia Tech vs. Tennessee. Who ya pullin' for?

These are all conundrums, questions with no easy answers. But that last one, known since the time of the ancient Greeks as the Tornado Game question, is a particularly thorny one.

The announcement of Georgia Tech playing Tennessee is the cosmos sending me a text that says, "Hey, puny human, a couple of months from now, you'll either wreck your car or get an IRS audit notification. We'll let you know which of these strikes our fancy on that date."

You then ask me which one I "pull for." As a rational puny human, I can't "pull for" either one. I can only try to draw the most possible contentment from my daily life during my remaining moments, then face my destiny like a man.

Yes, we are endowed with the freedom and will to act. When confronted by clear evil, of course, reasonable people ask, "What can I do to stop this abhorrent thing, this victory by one of Tech or Tennessee?" In this case, the answer is *nothing*. I have checked with both leagues and the venue where the event will transpire. It seems they're serious. The game is on, and cannot be stopped. The authorities are deaf to our philosophical pleas and appeals to their sense of values. They'll sell you a ticket, but they won't discuss its moral underpinnings. There seem to be no philosophy majors in ticket offices. Very annoying.

"Okee fine," you say, "I get all that. So—who ya pullin' for?"

You're not listening. As you can't stop an approaching storm, you don't ask which of its destructive forces to "pull for," the torrential winds or the floodwaters. That's crazy talk. You simply man up and batten down the hatches.

If Georgia Tech puts a beating on an SEC team on national TV, that's an occasion of hideous, soul-deep catastrophe for me, a nightmare of the human spirit, a throw-back-your-head-and-shout-WHY-at-the-heavens moment.

Yet if Tennessee wins a game, any game, ever, against any opponent, for any reason at all, and I mean this—that's an affront to all that is pure and healthy and wholesome in life. It's like making loud fart sounds in church while the children's choir is performing.

Tech-Tennessee? That's a guy much bigger than me walking up and saying, "Hey, buddy. I'm going to either smash your fingers with this concrete block, or, alternatively, bust your nose until all the little bones fall out. Please state your preference."

I'd rather not do that. Instead, I'll just man up and avert my fanly eyes. That's what I suggest for you, students of advanced-level philosophy. Spend time with your family before this game. Go out and savor the rays of sunshine. Play with a small child. Seize the day before nausea seizes you.

As Socrates said, drinking also helps.

Epilogue: It's a Hail Mary, Charlie Brown!

I f you're anything like me, you're painfully, disgustingly old. You were actually here on this earth and growing up in the 1960s.

It was a world in which aeroplanes flew overhead, and penicillin was conquering diseases, yet civilization stumbled onward without Facebook. By 1969, men would walk on the moon, yet our greatest cultural breakthrough, the "selfie," was still decades away.

You lived in a world where comics were a big deal. No, not *standup* comics. Not comic *books*. I'm talking about *newspaper comics*. A whole page of these every day, in beautiful black and white, and the ink came off on your fingers.

What? You don't remember newspapers either? As Charlie Brown would say, *Sigh*.

You've probably also forgotten when your mother and I would walk fifteen, twenty miles to school every day, through an icy tundra, eyes watchful for Indian ambush.

Then again, if you're one of those young whippersnappers of today, what with your loud hip hop music and your offensive body-piercings, you're probably not even reading this on paper. You're getting it through newfangled e-reader, audio download, or perhaps through aromatherapy. My great-grandchildren take in all their books through aromatherapy these days.

But there I go again, wandering from the topic. Did I doze off?

Ah, that's right—the 1960s. When we'd sit at the breakfast table and read the comics page, wiping the ink on our placemats while Dad perused the box scores and asked Mom about the big words in Furman Bisher's column.

Furman Bisher? See, he was—oh, never mind.

Our go-to comic strip was *Peanuts*, Charles Schulz's brilliant four panels of pre-postmodern angst. You could like it because you were a kid or because you were a cognitive psychotherapist. Charlie Brown, Linus, and the gang had huge heads and serious issues.

Peanuts had many iconic scenes:
- Snoopy vs. the Red Baron;
- Snoopy's happy dance;
- Linus waiting for the Great Pumpkin;
- Lucy's psychiatry booth (best nickel therapy in town).

But over the years, one image has etched itself most deeply into our cultural psyche: Lucy pulling the football away as Charlie Brown tries to boot it.

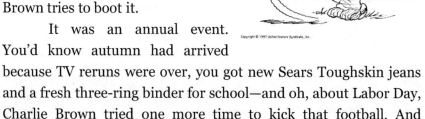

Copyright © 1997 United Feature Syndicate, Inc.

It was an annual event. You'd know autumn had arrived because TV reruns were over, you got new Sears Toughskin jeans and a fresh three-ring binder for school—and oh, about Labor Day, Charlie Brown tried one more time to kick that football. And whiffed.

Lucy always yanked the ball at the last possible second. Then Charlie Brown would float high in the air for an endless moment of existential despair before crashing to earth.

Lucy would then stand overhead, regard him like an insect she'd just stamped on, and cite some grain of bitter Zen truth. Lucy was never even flagged for taunting, because the ref didn't understand Zen or the bigger words in Furman Bisher's columns. And because hey, it was Charlie Brown. Suffering was his basic job description.

A laff riot, don't you agree? Nothing's funnier to us than the psychic pain of small children. Schulz once said, "You can't get comedy out of happiness."

But the joke in that strip was never in its cruelty; it was about the *inevitability* of it.

See, nobody made Charlie Brown take another run at that football. Ol' Chuck could have told Lucy where to stuff the football. He could have said, "Nope. That worked between 1953 and 1977, but this is 1978, and I'm not your pigeon."

Instead, he always fell for it—literally—because every year, he was susceptible to the siren song of hope. He'd take off on a sprint, saying, "This time is the one! This time I'll kick that thing past the Jumble and smack into Beetle Bailey's bunker."

Then: *Whump.* Once again, he was staring upward at Dennis the Menace, the strip up on the next floor, who was laughing his butt off. Charlie Brown, the goat of the comic page.

You know where I'm going with this, don't you?

Rolling Stone, of all magazines, actually published an article called *Good Grief: Georgia's Mark Richt is College Football's Charlie Brown*. It was right after the 2014 game in Columbia, when Todd Gurley wasn't given the ball on the goal line against South Carolina. A big victory was teed up for the Dawgs, and Spurrier had pulled the ball away *again*.

The Dawgnation shouted "Aaugh! You blockhead, Mark Richt!" *Rolling Stone* went so far as to point out that Richt had once injured his hip by falling off a child's swing while trying to impress his wife. Mark Richt, the goat of the sports section. In the SEC, he was the Charlie Browniest!

But we all know that *goat* is short for *scapegoat*—someone who unfairly shoulders the blame. You and I know it was never really about Richt or any particular coach, even Mike Bobo. There were plenty of AAUGH moments before those guys showed up, and we had some awful ones the first year after Richt departed for Miami. Charlie is a shade of Brown you can't wash away so easily.

What other group of fans recalls whole seasons by which Hail Mary they were victimized by that year? "Oh, 2013—year of the Auburn Tip-Six. And 2016, that's when we finally got a Hail Mary of our own against the Vols—then lost a few seconds later on a *counter*-Hail Mary."

Good grief!

Admit it. You remember the big moments by what That Guy Who Sits Behind you shouted at the time:

"Spike the ball, RICHT!"

"Give it to Gurley, RICHT!"

"Why did you squib it, RICHT?"

Slate.com offered a fascinating article on the history of Charlie Brown, Lucy, and the elusive placekick. They investigated all the annual strips, beginning in the early 1950s, and made several intriguing discoveries. Maybe a couple of these can even teach us something.

1. You're a Head Case, Charlie Brown!

Imagine this: In the beginning, Lucy wasn't the problem.

All right, she did pull the ball away that very first time, in 1952. She decided, at the last minute, she didn't want his dirty shoes griming up her nice, new ball. A woman is allowed to change her mind. What's important is that, in the same strip, she gave him another try—and this time, *she didn't pull the ball away!* He whiffed all on his own. Kid simply swung and he missed.

A bad break can take root and grow into an attitude. Over the years, the gag took on a life of its own. Lucy became a little meaner, and sure, wildly creative in her meanness. Charlie became a little more desperate. Lucy was the slumlord of whatever real estate existed between his ears.

Before long, Lucy knew, Charlie Brown knew, and the whole world knew what was going to happen. Charlie Brown was slowly trashing his psyche as well as establishing a lifetime of visits to the chiropractor. But he couldn't stop. He was locked in.

When things keep going wrong, sometimes we blame fate, history, the bounce of the ball. We say "God has it in for us." Larry Munson had a thing for "Old Lady Luck," and he wasn't talking about Lucy—though it's true she had to be close to his age by this time.

In 1990, Charlie Brown met a nice girl at camp, name of Peggy Jean. Definitely on the cute side. Girlfriend material. She smiled and offered to hold the football for him, but he was plagued by inner fears; terrified she'd morph into one more Lucy. When he declined her placeholding advances, Peggy Jean was offended and left camp. Sigh.

Come on, dude. God, fate, and Old Lady Luck aren't really interested in fixing football games. As Charlie Brown's comic page buddy, Pogo Possum, once said, "We have met the enemy, and he is us."

2. It's a Clean Slate, Charlie Brown!

Peanuts ended its run in February of 2000, when Schulz passed away. In the final placekicking episode, October 24 of the previous year (the week Georgia was preparing for another Jacksonville whiff-and-whump), Lucy didn't hold the football. Instead, she asked her little brother Rerun to do the job.

In an interesting move, the strip left open the question of whether he did that, and whether Charlie Brown finally nailed that sucker. We'll never know.

One thing about the future. It's always left open. I'd like to think Rerun, who seemed like a nice kid, held the ball, and toe finally met leather, and somewhere Charlie Brown is selling car insurance, rebuilding his lower back foundation, and is settled down happily with the Little Red-Headed Girl.

I'd also like to think Kirby Smart, who was a graduate assistant on that '99 team, will not be a rerun of the sadder traditions currently lingering around Georgia football.

As I write this, July has begun creeping toward August, and we know what that means. On the Dawgvent, the Charlie Browns of the world are preparing for another epic disappointment. Just because.

And a lot of other fans are thinking differently. They dare to hope. Like Charlie Brown, their hearts are beating faster, and they're stepping into a sprint. "This is it," they're telling themselves. "This time we nail it."

Whaddaya think? Big season or another clunker? Only sure thing is a lively conversation about that on the Vent.

Because that's how we get our kicks.

About the Author

Rob Suggs, known to true Americans as Saxondawg, has entrusted his soul to Georgia football for longer than you really want to know. He saw his first game during the administration of President Chester A. Arthur, when post-game traffic jams often consumed several weeks, due to stagecoach breakdowns.

President Arthur

Rob is an Atlanta native, from back in the day when actual natives populated Atlanta. His mother and father met at the University of Georgia, their love remaining true through the Wally Butts fifties, and they married during the off-week between Auburn and Tech.

Rob has been a cartoonist and author for many years, writing or collaborating on more than sixty books, including his own *Top Dawg: Mark Richt and the Revival of Georgia Football* (2008). He also co-authored *One Yard Short: Turning Your Defeats into Victories* with former NFL and Super Bowl coach Les Steckel (2006) as well as *Tenacious*, the story of Georgia high school coach Jeremy Williams and his personal fight with ALS and his son's spinal bifida.

As a Damn Fairly-Good Dawg, Rob provided the cover cartoon for *Georgia Bulldog* magazine's special 1980 National Championship issue. He spoke to the team in pregame chapel in 1990, on a day when the Dawgs upset Alabama. Rob's satirical work as Saxondawg has appeared since the advent of the famed Dawgvent fan site, where he was also press spokesman for the prophet Ooga, the Hunkering Hermit of Dawgly Lore.

Rob, with his wife, and two grown children, continue to hunker down in Atlanta, Georgia. Rob has arranged to have his body cryogenically frozen, so that he might be awakened to join in the festivities should the Dawgs ever win the whole blasted thing.

Find out more about Rob's work at:

www.robsuggs.com
www.saxondawg.com

If you enjoyed **Sax Attacks***,*
and you're into Christmas—
or if you're not particularly into Christmas,
but you do enjoy humorous prose about the
suffering of others, or if, actually, none of
that's your thing, but you'd like to help Rob
pay some bills and reclaim his signed,
limited edition Barbara Dooley bobblehead
from the pawn shop—any reason is cool,
Rob doesn't care—then be sure to read . . .

CHRISTMAS ATE MY FAMILY

Rob and Christmas are locked in yet another deadly struggle. They've had had their differences in the past. Now, as an alleged dad, Rob is dead set on delivering his two kids the perfect Christmas morning. But what about that wildly popular toy, for which he must face off against hordes of other snarling parents? What about the small son who insists on giving his requests personally to Santa? Then there's Rob's horrifying Yuletide trip to the gym. Navigating from one holiday fiasco to another, he carries us on a wild Christmas journey, vividly and with occasional honesty. Put the humbug back in Christmas with this new holiday classic.

Christmas Ate My Family by Rob Suggs

Available in paper and ebook from Amazon.com
Or just hunt down Rob and ask.

GET INTO THE GAME

Nobody covers the Dawgs like us.

- The **best coverage out there** when it comes to Georgia sports: news, photos, interviews, video, podcasts. **Nobody else comes close.**
- **We're there first** with the latest recruiting scoops.
- **The famous Dawgvent,** where true Dawgs break it all down, 365/24/7. Meet your new best friends.
- **The Rivals network,** unrivaled for sports coverage.

TRY IT FREE FOR 3 MONTHS
New subscribers only.

1 MONTH FREE, CURRENT MEMBERS
Who purchased this book.

USE COUPON CODE "SAXONBOOK"

www.uga.rivals.com/sign_up

75344696R00118

Made in the USA
Columbia, SC
19 August 2017